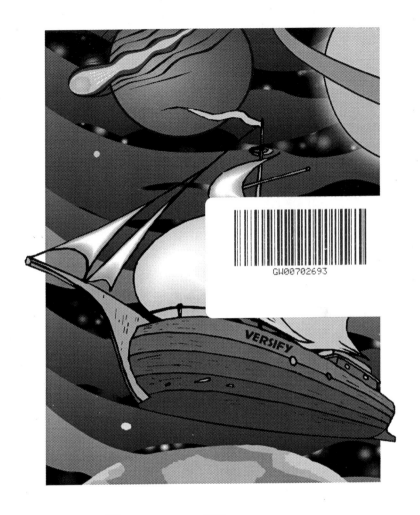

POETIC VOYAGES
BEDFORDSHIRE

Edited by Simon Harwin

First published in Great Britain in 2001 by
YOUNG WRITERS
Remus House,
Coltsfoot Drive,
Peterborough, PE2 9JX
Telephone (01733) 890066

HB ISBN 0 75433 088 5
SB ISBN 0 75433 089 3

FOREWORD

Young Writers was established in 1991 with the aim to promote creative writing in children, to make reading and writing poetry fun.

This year once again, proved to be a tremendous success with over 88,000 entries received nationwide.

The Poetic Voyages competition has shown us the high standard of work and effort that children are capable of today. It is a reflection of the teaching skills in schools, the enthusiasm and creativity they have injected into their pupils shines clearly within this anthology.

The task of selecting poems was therefore a difficult one but nevertheless, an enjoyable experience. We hope you are as pleased with the final selection in *Poetic Voyages Bedfordshire* as we are.

CONTENTS

Jamie Gray	80
Rabia Saghir	80
Abbas Ali	81
Shohidur Rahman	81
Imran Tariq	82
Simone Robinson	82
Maryam Bibi	83
Ateeq Choudhury	83
Jessica Hunter	84
Sameena Shakur	85

Pirton Hill Junior School

Bhipashah Yasmin	85
Sharelle Bailey	86
Renate O'Connor	86
Paul Young	87
Latifah Cain-Greaves	87
Nico Gonsalves	88
Sheraz Ahmed	88
Rahbiya Chaudaury	89
Emily Goldney	89
Ryan Derby	90
Liam Connolly	90
Rio Sreedharan	91
Hannah Hunt	92
Danielle Sullivan	92
Kimberley	93
Jodi Roach	93
Sitara Ahmed	94
Daniel Hynes	94
Stephen Avery	95
Nathan James	95
Kirsty Warren	96
Shaneen Simmonds	96
Roshni Sagoo	97
Daniel Davies	98
Michael Reed	98
Leanna Atkinson	98

St Margaret Of Scotland RC Junior School

Louise Davie	139
Ben Ryan	140
Naomi Cunningham	140
Laura Catling	141
Kayleigh Kerins	141
Stephanie Rankin	142
Kelly Gethin	142
Megan Moorhouse	143
Amy O'Neill	143
Laura Murphy	144
Jodie Roberts	144
Sophie Amos	145
Paul Coy	146
Sinéad Hegarty	146
Ruth Baker	147
Peter Gleasure	147
Liam Reddan`	148
Diasy Monaghan	148
James Sherry	149
Mary-Ann Cheshire	149
Séamus Griffin	150
Emily Donnellan	150
Niamh Patton	151
Joella Forsyth	151
David Scott	152
Katie Sears	152
Rebecca Byrne	153
Kayleigh McLaughlin	153
Alessandra Doogan	154
Maria Cortese	155
Luke Sears	156
Daniel Panepinto	156
Ziedo Solomon	157
Claire Legg	158
James McGuinness	159
Leana Brady	160
Trixie Thomas	161

The Poems

ON A VOYAGE
(Skate rap)

I'm on a voyage
To learn to kickflip
I'll Ollie up
Then spin the board
And pray to the Lord
Steady my feet
And take a great leap
Over the ramp I go
The board is dangerously low
I reach for it
It's going in the pit
No I catch the board
And thank the Lord
Land on the ramp
Then skate to the camp.

Freddy Corkett (10)
Alameda Middle School

MY CAT FLEW UP TO SPACE ONE DAY

My cat flew up to space one day
to see what he could see.
And when he started floating up
he then shouted *'Wee!'*
I saw him on the rings of Saturn,
And also eating Mars.
But then he flew away that day
I'd say he went too far.

Alexandra Gummery (10)
Alameda Middle School

Voyage Through My Mind

Start at the ear
Off we go
Slow and steady
Woooooo.
Chugging along
through my mind
I wonder what
We'll find.
This looks
like the picture gallery
there's my mum and dad.
My friends, oh no
there's my brother.
Why is he here?
Chugging along
through my mind.
I wonder what
we will find.
Here we are
at the memory bank arrr
My mum's birthday
in three days.
Chugging along
through my mind.
I wonder what we
will find.
That was short
but good, out we gooooo
Woooooo.

Michael Rayner (11)
Alameda Middle School

SPACE ATTACK

I was watching telly
When . . .
My head started spinning
Then . . . then . . .
The television sucked me in the screen
I started to shout but no one could hear me
Help!
Help!
Help!
I saw I was in space
Then I saw a space ship
Then . . . Then . . . Bang!
They attacked us
Quick . . . out, out, out!
I jumped out I wondered what would happen,
I fell
Down, down, down
But
I want to go home
I wish
I wish
I could go home
It did not work
I tried again
It worked
It worked
I'm out.

Melanie Cole (11)
Alameda Middle School

The Haunted House

When I woke
A voice spoke
The wind squealed
As I kneeled.

The door squeaked
The tap leaked
I smelt musty
or was it rusty?

I heard a creak
Should I speak?
I fell to my knees
And lost my keys.

I found a door
What do you think I saw?
Was it a man?
Then I ran.

Up some stairs
Then I stared
It was my sister Bella
In the cellar.

Kelly Lawes (10)
Alameda Middle School

Life Of A Guinea-Pig

I think about my Guinea-Pig,
She doesn't have much fun,
It's only in the Summer time,
She gets out in her run.

In the Winter when it's cold
She gets extra tlc
And when it freezes over
I think she misses me.

Caroline Howard (11)
Alameda Middle School

A VOYAGE ON A SHIP

We set sail
in a stormy gale.

I went all pale
So I fetched some ale.

I made a sandwich, bread and cheese
Sat outside, enjoyed the breeze.

The wind blew and blew
We lost more and more crew.

Then we crashed
and I was down there too.

The water was pink
as we started to sink.

Then it turned red
as I lost my head.

We hit the bottom
Now dead, but not forgotten.

Edward Skinner (10)
Alameda Middle School

MY HAMSTER

My hamster sleeps all day my hamster comes out at night
My hamster plays around my hamster runs around
My hamster plays in his wheel
My hamster makes a mess
My hamster is so cute you can't resist
His beady eyes are so cute
He puts his sawdust on the floor
So when you come in the door you
You will see sawdust on the floor
They scamper around at night
If you put them together they might fight
My hamster's name is Patch he is very hard to catch
He chews and bites the bars at night to keep his teeth
Just right
Gleaming white.

Anna Leece (10)
Alameda Middle School

A VOYAGE THROUGH LIFE!

First of all I was a tiny baby and I couldn't see
Then one day I grew and grew till I was sixteen
After that I began to get older
Then when I was nineteen I fell and dislocated
my shoulder.
Then I decided to be helpful and be a vet
And ended up with twenty pets
After that I became an old lady
But I still had fun with my neighbour Sadie
Then one very sad sad day
I simply just passed away.

Robyn Adams (10)
Alameda Middle School

WHAT AM I?

I start off as a puny bug, I wouldn't harm a fly,
This is a poem about my life, And how the world flies by.
I used to be a tiny egg, as small as small can be,
Now the warmer weather's here, I'm sheltered by a tree,
I leave my egg my body's long, my skin is white and red,
I walk around a little while, but then I go to bed.

When I awake the blackbird sings,
Look at my back, now I have wings.
I look all around, my eyes are a blur,
There isn't a sound not even a stir.
I spread my wings wide, they're red, blue and green,
I'm the most beautiful creature you've ever seen,
My journey has ended as you can see,
Now have a guess what could I be?

Abigail Jones (11)
Alameda Middle School

VOYAGE POEM TO GET MY PUPPY

This is my puppy,
He costs too much for me,
So I got my mummy to buy him for me.
To get him we went to Scotland
We flew over the Jodrell bank
And landed at the breeder's house,
We picked up the puppy and called him Zorro,
Then came the boring part, driving part,
Driving Home.

Faith Phillips (10)
Alameda Middle School

VOYAGE THROUGH MY BROTHER'S LIFE

When my brother was a kitten,
Our mum died,
A human fed us so we survived.

When my brother was four months old,
People took him away,
He was my favourite brother,
I cried that very day.

A month later when I was five months old,
Some people took me away,
I cried hoping my brothers and me would be OK.

When I got to my new home,
A year later when I went out to play,
I saw a cat in the distance,
I went close to make a friend,
I saw it was my *brother,*
Then I never cried again!

Chloe Pearson (10)
Alameda Middle School

LIFE OF A DOG

When I was born
and came to this world,
my tail was wagging
and sometimes curled.

I like the food I always have
I copied the cats to catch
I like my doghouse
It's very comfortable
and I've got a really good name
for me it's Mable.

When my owner is very sad
I can feel the pain,
but when I am with her,
she won't feel the pain again!

When years are passing,
I get very old
I have many friends,
that look like me
and when I die
I am free!

Joanne Yu (10)
Alameda Middle School

LIFE AS A BABY

When I was a baby I was very funny
I liked to suck my dummy.

I wore a nappy
and I was very wacky.

I made up a game called clappy
and I was very happy

I liked my dinner
and the doorbell was a ringer

I looked out of the window
and saw somebody doing the limbo

I had a pot of cookies
and somebody went to the bookies

I was a very good grinner
because I was a winner.

Shane Moore (11)
Alameda Middle School

ROLLER COASTER

What am I doing here?
I must be mad!
Queuing for so long!
I'm only a little lad.
It only takes a sec
that voyage to the beginning
my pulse racing
my face facing the drop the twist the loop amazing
my face is white my nails have gone
I'm going to be scared all along.
What it's finished?
Oh that's not too bad!
Can we go again dad, please dad, dad?

Laurie Cornwell (10)
Alameda Middle School

WINTER COMING AUTUMN GOING

The autumn is going
The winter is coming
The snow is falling
The wind is calling
The leaves are rustling
The trees are hovering
the grass is no longer green
And the flowers are no longer seen.
The snowmen are white
And the days are never light
But soon spring will be here
And there will be no fear
The flowers will soon bloom
Right into my room.

Christina Dixon (10)
Alameda Middle School

TOGETHER FOREVER

We met in a barn
on a sunny summer's day.
It was both her
and my birthday.

My little black friend
padded over to me.
She nudged my leg
and purred at my knee.

I bent and lifted her
into my arms.
She meowed so cutely,
I fell for her charms.

All her whiskers are
completely black,
and she looks like a sphinx
a type of Egyptian cat.

My little black kitten
Smudge is her name.
And we are the best friends
that have ever been made.

She sits on my neck to
warm me up after a cold day,
and I cuddle her
in just the right way.

The instant we met
we knew, we foresaw,
that we would be best friends
for evermore . . .

Maria-Rose Eves-Down (11)
Alameda Middle School

LIFE OF A RABBIT

My name is Flopsy and I am one year of age,
I have a sister and her name is Paige.

I've got ears that are floppy and I'm very very soppy.

I enjoy playing in the garden, I go for a run and
have lots of fun.

When I am poorly my owners take me to the vets,
Where I see lots of other pets.

When I'm alone I'm more fearful but when I'm
with others I'm cheerful.

At the end of the day I make myself clean and
fall asleep having nice dreams.

Charlotte South (10)
Alameda Middle School

RHYMING PIRATES

I walked on board the ship and set sail.
What is that? Just a nail.
When I was out to sea I saw plenty of sea creatures.
It made a change from learning from teachers.
Moments later I was boarded by pirates who liked a rhyme.
To be boarded by pirates this isn't the time.
'We three pirates are searching for gold
We have some but it's rather old.
We want some more as you may see
So if you've got some give it to my friends and me.'
They searched the ship high and low,
but of course no success.
Finally the pirates left leaving my ship in a terrible mess.

James Parsons (11)
Alameda Middle School

MYSTIFYING TIME

Walking through the playground gate,
I get that feeling I am late.
I hear a scream, my head turns back,
The sound comes first, a thud a whack.
Someone grabs me by the hand,
Concrete turns to squidgy sand.
The scream has gone, instead there's waves,
I'm on a beach with rocks and caves.
I try to run my legs stick fast,
Now I'm sinking back to past.
Yesterday comes floating near,
'Oh I'm so glad that I am here.'
For now I'm here to right the wrong,
I told my friend I'd gone for long.
The school bell rings, I start to run,
Back to school to have some fun!

Alice Perry (10)
Alameda Middle School

MY VOYAGE

We set sail on the ocean blue,
We had a very bad voyage and a cut-throat
                                crew.
We sailed for days on nice calm seas
then we hit a storm that shook our knees.
We took down the sails
and started baling out.
Then all of a sudden we heard a shout.
We'd run aground just off the shore
We'd make it there,
and the storm was no more.

William Allingham (10)
Alameda Middle School

VOYAGE THROUGH LIFE AND SUFFERINGS

At first I was a baby,
Really very tiny.
I covered myself in shoe polish
And people said 'Oh Blimey!'
For that black, disgusting shoe polish
Had made me very shiny.

But that shine didn't last for long
Because when I became two
My parents took me for a birthday treat
Off to the zoo
And they weren't very pleased when I
Rolled in brown goo.

After that I started growing
And by the time I was ten
I'd put on loads of weight
And was bigger than Big-Ben!
And as lonely as a person can be
I played alone in my den.

As I got older I made new friends
Who stuck up for me, of course.
But I was happy even though I got teased,
'Cause I plodded around with such force.
Maybe was a little clumsy
And acted like a drunken horse.

I didn't suffer much then, but
When I was twenty
I got ill and became diabetic.
And what was worse I got self conscious
And also became anorexic.
So I spent a lot of time in hospital
Feeling very sick.

A little while later, still in hospital
I was a terrible wreck
Then one day I had a stroke
And all the doctors were shouting
'Oh goodness, oh hec!'
'Get me the medicine, get me the pills!'
And doctors scuttled everywhere,
All hands on deck.

After I got well, life was pretty straightforward,
But one very dull day when I was eighty three
I was sitting in my garden
Thinking how great life could be
When two very fat robbers
Leapt out at me!
I screamed then fainted,
And my spirit became free . . .

Jennie Randall (10)
Alameda Middle School

SPACE

I was walking through space singing to me,
I looked up above and what did I see,
two big aliens smiling at me,
they said they would like to be friends and would I
take tea?
So they took me to their home in the Apollo 3,
and what did I see?
A little baby alien trying to jump on me,
I had space food for tea.
And went back home in the Apollo 3.

Glenn McGrath (10)
Alameda Middle School

IMAGINARY LAND

I'm going on a voyage to an imaginary land
I'm going to the shed to make a flying van.
When it's ready I'll start my voyage.
I can't wait to go it will be just like magic.
When I get there it will be just right
I hope it isn't late in the night.
Now I'm in this amazing land.
I can hear an echo of a band.
I wander around and find a beach
I can't wait to eat a juicy peach.

When I get home I'll wake up
and find it was just a dream.

Thomas Busler (11)
Alameda Middle School

A BIG STEP TO LIFE

Where am I?
Where have I gone?
Who's that person?
Is that my mum?
I'm really cold,
I want to go home.
I need my friends to gut the bone,
It's a new adventure,
I must be prepared,
Get rid of my nerves.
Stop being scared.

I'm a baby now I've got a new life!

Anna Vesty (11)
Alameda Middle School

THROUGH THE PARK

Through the gate
I go, I go.

The wind, the wind blows in my
hair.
I don't care.

The dog, the dog jumps in the air
I don't care.

The kid, the kid shouts that's not fair
I don't care.

The man, the man has no hair
I don't care.

Through the gate
I go, I go.

Edward Sharpe (11)
Alameda Middle School

MY SEA VOYAGE

I went on a voyage on a ship on the sea.
To visit places new and old.
I saw in Barcelona where Linford Christie
won his Gold.
I went to Pisa to see the leaning tower.
I then went to Rome where the Pope has the power.
The Apes in Gibraltar were sitting on the rock,
Every day was exciting, a different place to dock.

Chris Carey (11)
Alameda Middle School

PEOPLE

Some are funny,
Some are crude,
Some are bright and sunny,
Some are rude,
Some are emotional,
Some are soppy,
And others like to cheat and copy.
Some love music,
Some get angry and start to lose it.
Some like to get on,
Opposites chat,
Some like the dogs,
Others like the cat.
Some always punishes,
One never flaggs.

However you are,
You are a person,
There's no boundary and there's no bar
Of how you are.

Jaz Mawson (10)
Alameda Middle School

MY LITTLE BOAT

I set off in my little boat to discover places new
Across the seas, with the cool calm breeze
And the whales and dolphins too.

One night a great storm blew up
And broke my mast in two
My boat it crashed against the rocks
And sank into the ocean blue.

I swam and swam to reach the shore
All through the cold dark night
And then the land was suddenly there
It was such a lovely sight.

Laura E Mayes (11)
Alameda Middle School

MY LIFE

When I was born
I used to yawn
When I was one
I used to suck my thumb
When I was two
I used to go to the loo!
When I was three
I got stung by a bee
When I was four
I could open a door
When I was five
I went for a dive
When I was six
I ate my first Twix
When I was seven
I wished I was eleven
When I was eight
I had a nice mate
When I was nine
I was growing up fine
When I was ten
I went swimming with my brother Ben.

Tom Gregory (10)
Alameda Middle School

MORNING CALL

Good morning my dear
I hope you are here,
And if you're not I hope you're well,
Your journey today,
Will take you away,
On aeroplane, train and none else.
The first call's Japan,
A must for your Nan,
And if she's well we will leave.
Our next stop is Chile,
The dresses are frilly,
But don't be too friendly you see,
We leave for Madagascar,
This trip is a fiasca,
But worth the education for me.
And if we have time,
We will pick up a dime,
And find a place to stop for tea.
And on the way home,
You may use a phone,
To see if they're ready for me.

Louisa Anderson (11)
Alameda Middle School

THE SHIP OF FRIENDS

As we sailed across the sea
The cheers of glee
From the pirates
When they thought they'd stole our treasure.

We don't care.
Because we have something we can share
This is something nobody can take
But someone can make . . .

This is our friendship,
We'll always be sailing
On the friendly sea
On the *Ship of Friends.*

Laura Wood (11)
Alameda Middle School

POETIC VOYAGES

I sailed the seas of verbs and nouns,
To find the right phonetic sounds.
I sailed through adverbs and like
To find some conjunctions on a bike.
I found I'd come to the land of phrase,
Where people speak in lots of ways.
I shouted 'You! Get off that bike,'
But And and Meanwhile
Just laughed at me with a big fat smile.
I found a noun washed up ashore,
Its body was all red and raw.
'I'm car' it spluttered
'I'm me' I muttered.
I went to the zoo and looked about
'Oi!' Keeper said 'You litter lout!
Stop scattering words, or you'll be out.'
I picked them up, and then walked on,
Then I found my noun had gone.
'Twas elephant I found by name
O great! My virtue had then came.
For ph was a phonetic sound,
Then I set off, homeward bound.

Timothy Hele (10)
Alameda Middle School

THE VOYAGE THROUGH MY LIFE AS A FISH

I started as a little baby.
Me, my brothers and my sisters.
When they brought me I was three
                         weeks old.
There were seven of us altogether,
which became nine when two new
members joined the family.
People came, people stared, I just swam
                         and swam.
They fed me food that was very nice.
They brought me toys to swim through.
They cleaned my tank.
They brought me fresh weed to help me
                         breathe.
That's all I have to say now I'm too busy
                         swimming away.

Katie Jarvis (10)
Alameda Middle School

THE VOYAGE

The wild waves lashed against the boat,
The rain was pouring down,
The crew were desperate, frightened, scared,
What if they would drown?

The sails were flailing in the wind,
A muffled cry was heard,
The sails had ripped and flown away,
Like a glistening bird.

The ship, by now, a useless wreck,
Was heading for the rocks.
The crew looked white, tired, ill,
In their stripey smocks.

At last the great ship reached its doom,
And smashed against the crag,
The voyage was finished, the sailors gone,
The ship, their homes and bags.

Emma Mackley (10)
Alameda Middle School

MY VOYAGE TO THE SEA

I was going on a journey to the sea with the crew,
It was a nice sunny day before it started raining,
The crew weren't very nice to me for when I asked them
for a cup of tea.
They laughed and said haven't you any money?
I was so angry, I went in another room and slammed the door
behind me.

When I sat down in that room,
A man came to me and said 'How about a cup of tea?'
Although he was fat and ugly,
I still said yes, for I was very hungry and thirsty,
That man seemed the opposite of the crew I first spoke to.

I drank the tea and gave the glass back to the man.
It was getting dark but I didn't feel like going to sleep, so
I watched the sea.
The waves were very big.
I could just see the fish in the dark,
Then after a little while we were there.

Shivanee Nakum (8)
Broadmead School

INSIDE MY BODY

Travelling through my body
on a magic carpet.

What do I see?
Many strange but exciting things.

No-one knows but while I'm travelling
on the magic carpet I'm still walking
through the Arndale.

Now the big me is in Woolworths but that's
boring because that's the big one.

The little one is still on the magic carpet.

I'm passing over the heart and
Aaaahhhha!

That was me sliding down my arm.
I think it's time to go back to just having one me.

Out through the mouth, and the tiny me disappeared.
Forever.

Hayley Smith (9)
Broadmead School

UNDERGROUND

In the murky underground
Are beggars lying all around
Cobwebs, litter everywhere
People pass without a care.

In the noisy underground
Peace and calm is never found
People rushing to and fro
People queuing row on row.

In the gloomy underground
On the track is out of bound
Full of darkness on the track
Every few minutes the train comes back.

In the murky underground
Are beggars lying all around
Cobwebs, litter everywhere
People pass without a care.

Freya Bass (10)
Broadmead School

OUT OF THE AEROPLANE WINDOW

I looked
Out of
The Aeroplane
Window
Blue and white the sky.
Sun shining in my eyes.
Noises of the other aeroplane
Made me really scared.
I close my eyes and ears until
The plane went off really far.
Now I got really scared
We were
Landing
But I
Was
Fine.

Rakhee Parmar (10)
Broadmead School

TRAVELLING

I like ships,
but only a bit.

Planes are cool,
but only ones with a swimming pool.

Cars are okay,
but I prefer to play.

Wobbling rollerblades,
when you're wearing shades.

Horses are slow,
not even faster than a crow.

I don't like walking,
I prefer talking.

Bikes are my kind,
and aren't hard to find.

Motorbikes are fast,
and don't end up last.

This is the end,
come on friend.

Nico Bains
Broadmead School

TO MARS ... (OR NOT!)

Off I go,
I'm off to Mars
I can see those shining stars!

Oh No!
Crash! Bang! Boom!
This wasn't Mars it was The Land of Doom!

'Oh no a beast!' I said,
This must be my last ride,
Is it?

'Hello' the beast said to me,
He wasn't horrid, he was friendly,
Phew!

The beast said he would throw me to Mars,
In one of his giant Ferrari cars,
He threw me!

Here I am about to land,
On the ground ...
Mars!

This isn't Mars,
Not at all.
Was it worth, to come straight back to Earth?

Vinesh Patel (11)
Broadmead School

A TRAIN VOYAGE

When I was on the train
I sat down
The weather was sunny
And it was a bumpy ride.

A few miles across the track
It got foggy and the train slowed down
Then I started to get bored
Every thirteen miles the weather changed.

I looked outside
Black was the sky
I got very scared
But then I was not scared
That was because it was sunny again.

Aidan Kennedy (9)
Broadmead School

THE VOYAGE BACK IN TIME

Blue wavy sea splashing on Me
Fish eating other fish.

The crew getting ill but we forgot the pills.
All the food went crumbly.
The wine bottles smashed.
Part of the crew were being sick.
The crew was rocking back and forth.
Wondering if they will survive.
Praying and weeping.
But only a few survived.

Mandheer Mangat (10)
Broadmead School

A JOURNEY TO WONDERLAND?

Falling into dreamworld
Pushing cobwebs from my side
I travel on my journey to the dark depths of my mind
This side is all grey and boring full with pain and sorrow
But as I travel on colours spray from here to tomorrow
Bright and happy I want to stay
Where dolphins fly and people say
'Goodnight' instead of 'Gooday'
I travel further on to find
I've really left my world behind
Round and round
Up and down
I start to fall and almost drown
I crawled out the water onto the bank
And started to walk well I ran
Until I tripped over and scraped my knees
Past me blew a cool soft breeze
I looked up and saw a door
I stood up and felt a claw
Grab me from behind
It was getting creepy in my mind.
I turned around and it was gone
On the floor a gold key shone
So I picked it up in the door it fitted
Then I turned the handle and pushed
My way back out of Wonderland
And back into my own warm bed
Was it a dream?
          I wonder?

Rosie Plane (11)
Broadmead School

MY FUNNY VOYAGE WITH AN ANNOYING BIRD

When I was in a ship on my voyage,
Sailing on the sea,
What did I see buzzing past me,
A disgusting dirty furry little bee.

Later on I was sitting staring at the sky,
Soon a little bird passed my little arm,
and then flew around my head.

Suddenly that little bird came by again,
and splat on my head and my clothes what did I see?
I was covered in white stuff,
I had no choice but to pour water all over me.

Soon I was tucked up for the night in my bed,
I went into a deep sleep while I was resting my head.
Suddenly the same bird woke me up,
I had such a fright.
The bird flew around my head and said,
'The ship is about to tip over and sink to the bottom of the sea.'
I jumped out of the ship and soon found out that the bird had
                                        tricked me..
Soon I thought of a plan to get my own back,
on that clever little bird.
I thought of saying that a hunter's coming and he's going to
                                        shoot you,
but he didn't fly away.
We soon reached land, and I sent the bird away.
But the little bird came back another day.
Soon what I said to the bird came true,
a hunter did come and shoot the bird,
I then shouted with glee!
Hip Hip *Hooray!*

Jayna Gandhi (9)
Broadmead School

ZONKO HERE WE COME!

Here we are on our way,
Going through the Milky Way,
And on an endless black sea,
Behind galaxies are merely streams.

Here we are among the stars,
Galaxies near and far.
Now we've missed the planet Ronkers.
We will not all go bonkers.

Zonko's our destination,
We've no time for recreation.
Here we are going through space,
We will win the big race.

Hold on we're going the wrong way
Why am I seeing a shining ray,
North, South, East or West,
Oh no we're in a mess!

Here we are in rubbish land,
Oh no a good looking man!
Oh phew he just ran,
Aaah there's a lamb!

Oh no such scary things,
A house, a mouse and even a grouse!
Oh quickly get on the ship,
Aaah I've got two rips!

Quickly look there is Zonko,
Land us down Mr Rumko,
Oh look there is Funko's,
We can dance if we land,
Yes yahoo we're first man.

Jeevan Sandher (10)
Broadmead School

THE RAFT

Get some wood from the forest
We're going to build a raft!
Get the wood and the stool
I will get the tools.

I'm jolly well proud
With our perfect ride.
Let's take it to the Ocean.

Pack food and clothes
here we go!

We are out to sea
It's not rough but it will get tough.
This sea is getting rough and tough
hold onto the log.

Here comes a wave!

Here we are bobbing on the sea
No one else for us to see
Are we lost?
Oh no here comes some
Rocks!
hold onto the log.

Where are we
I can't see
Look we're on
an Island . . .?

Jassie Pile (11)
Broadmead School

FLOWERS

Flowers are beautiful
They are so colourful
They're everything to me
They're all I ever dream about
Well! These days.

Do you like flowers?
They're pretty like candy
You say 'He loves me or
He loves me not'
They all sit there in pots.

Not all of them in pots
Some are left in the ground
Because they need soil
That's the way they grow
Getting bigger, just like us.

I can't see many flowers, you know
That's because it's winter.
They sleep in the ground
Waiting for spring
When they grow again and say 'Hello'

But in my mind, they're always there
My favourite are tulips.
There's a magic in flowers
They turn sadness to joy
And you can tell someone that you care.

I love flowers so much
I have a bunch of them in my mind
They stay there always
Something special
In many sorts of ways.

Jasmin Choudhury (10)
Denbigh Junior School

MY BROTHER

My brother is so mean to me
I hope I have no more
I don't know how he was when he was born
But he's different than before.

He was so kind when I was little
And I was really pleased
But now he is so different
And now I just get teased.

He comes into my room
And will always disturb me,
He touches all my stuff
And is as silly as can be.

Whenever he borrows something of mine
He always loses it
I get all cross and shout at him
Then I get all the hits.

But now that he has left home
I thought it would be much better
But I guess I really miss him
When he sent me a letter.

Fatema Khatun (10)
Denbigh Junior School

WHAT IS LOVE?

Love is something that you feel
when you see that special someone.
Love can be good and make you feel happy
Love can be bad and make you feel sad.
But if you ask me
I think that sort of love is a waste of time.

Some people love pop groups
People love their families
Some people love their pets
Some people love their teachers
But if you're like me
The only thing I love is . . .

Chocolate!

Jazbah Ahmed (10)
Denbigh Junior School

ABOUT MY BROTHER

I hate my brother, he pulls my hair
He's only five years old.
I call him Midget, he gets all stressed
He calls me Midget back.
I laugh at him. 'How can I be a midget,
I'm not short like you?'
He goes and sulks and cries at mum,
Then I get all the blame.
Mum tells me off.
'It's not my fault,
I didn't start the fight.'
'Oh be quiet!' she tells me,
'You always say that.'
'But mum, it's the truth,' I try to explain,
As my brother just sits there laughing.
Oh how I hate my brother, he always pulls my hair.
He's only five years old,
And life just isn't fair!

Reda Zahra (9)
Denbigh Junior School

BULLY

Calling people stupid names,
Never thinking about what you say
You stand and hurt them every day
Even when they laugh and play.

B.U.L.L.Y
Bully people, make them cry
B.U.L.L.Y
You'll get punished, if you try.

Swearing, hurting, hitting too,
What have they ever done to you?
They've got feelings. Don't you care?
Treating them that way, it's just not fair.

B.U.L.L.Y
Bully people, make them cry
B.U.L.L.Y
You'll get punished, if you try.

I got bullied in my short life,
One day they stabbed me with a knife
Now you see I'm not alive.
Have you seen my picture and stood and cried?

B.U.L.L.Y
Bully people, they will cry.
B.U.L.L.Y
You'll get punished, so never try.

Nosheen Shaheen (11)
Denbigh Junior School

THE STARS

Shine, shine little stars
Looking like little candles
Shining, shining all night long
Small and bright and wonderful to look at.
Little angels in the sky
Twinkling like little specks of fireworks.
And when it's day
You go away, and I don't see you any more
Until the sun goes down and
The moon comes up
Then I see the twinkling stars again
Twinkling, twinkling, little stars.

Aruj Kayani (10)
Denbigh Junior School

STRANGE MORNING

Today I woke up, my shoes walked away.
I was amazed
I went to the bathroom, my brush walked away,
I was amazed.
I put on my uniform, my socks were not there,
I can't stop them running away.
I go downstairs for breakfast, my cereal runs away,
Oh good, I'm still asleep, and it's all a dream!

Sana Ahmed (10)
Denbigh Junior School

GOD'S GARDEN

I have a lot of friends who are all different colours and sizes.
Some are short, some are tall. Some are big, some are slim.
But all that really matters are that they are my friends.
It is the same with God's garden.
The world is his garden and all the different coloured people around
us are his flowers that are still coming each year.
He loves each of those flowers the same, young or old, girl or boy.
So let this poem show you that at least one person will always love you.
Even if you don't believe him he will believe in you.

Danielle Lizaitis (10)
Ferrars Junior School

ICE CREAM

Ice cream's cold
Ice cream's nice
Ice cream's nasty
Ice cream's pricey.

Some are brown
Some are pink
Some are yellow
Some are white
Nevertheless
I like them all
Ice cream
Ice cream
You're welcome in my door.

Tarkan Kranda (11)
Ferrars Junior School

THE SUN, CLOUDS AND ANGRY LIGHTNING

The sun is a circle of fire going round and round.
The sun is a yellow daisy growing to its full height
                              in the sun's garden.

Clouds are tufts of candyfloss floating in the sky.
Clouds of fluffy shades, pink, white and grey reflecting the
                                                    day.

Lightning crashing around, a dog barking and attacking
Lightning smashing down houses as if they are bits of
                                                    Lego.

Michael Janes (10)
Ferrars Junior School

LOVE POTION

A heart of a beautiful lovely girl
A bucket full of flowers
A golden string of hair.

A heart full of love
A Cupid with an arrow.
A feather full of love.

But all it needs is
You my love.
And love forever
Not forgetting
True love.

Kerdean Cyrus (11)
Ferrars Junior School

MY POEM (IF I HAVE ONE)

I'm trying to make up a poem,
My sister is telling me how.
My cat is really annoying me,
By (right in my ear) saying 'meow'.

Maybe a poem about the gobledygools,
Maybe about monster pips.
Maybe a horror about my sister dancing,
Like the way she moves her hips.

I've got an idea for a poem,
As I look over what I have done.
I'll jut write this out all over again,
And name it 'My Poem (if I have one)'

Andrew Esson (10)
Ferrars Junior School

THE STARS

The stars are like tiny diamonds
twinkling in the sky.
In the night they light up and
become so bright.
So if you see a diamond you'll know it's
                    just a star or is it . . .?
I shall never know or shall I?
If I could I would go out to space
and find out, but I can't.
Maybe someday . . . maybe someday.

Adam Broughton (10)
Ferrars Junior School

THE THREE MEAN CATS

The Cheetah is a streak of lightning
Flashing across the ground
His teeth are daggers
Stabbing into prey when it's found.

The Lion is a phantom disappearing in the night
Dodging out of his prey's sight.
He's a flame
That plays his own game.

The Tiger's swords slash through flesh
It gives him dinner
The prey is stuck like glue
Because the tiger's the winner.

David Holloway (9)
Ferrars Junior School

TAKING OFF

We're taking off,
I'm saying goodbye.
We're up so high in the sky.

I see the beautiful things
the birds, the sun and lots of other
                              things.
We're in the sky so high, high, high.

We see the tropical sea while we eat.
We're in the sky so very high.

We see the golden beach down below.
The people are waving to us.
We are waving back.

Maverick Fuller (9)
Ferrars Junior School

STORM

The storm is a thunderbolt
with lightning as a flash of light,
The Gods strike on us,
As we get stabbed by their yellow ray of
                                        light.

We make a bolt for shelter before we get
                                struck upon,
Bang, bash, crash, he got us all by hitting the
                                        tree.

Bang, boom the thunder had defeated the lightning,
but he was only wishing,
We were safe -
But we could still hear the thunder crashing on our roof,
The tiles fell off,
The lightning didn't give up,
Then the God's anger struck our house and
                                it was on fire.

Harry Peel (9)
Ferrars Junior School

THUNDER AND LIGHTNING

Thunder and lightning is God playing his drums
                                and tambourines.
He doesn't play well he plays badly.

Crash! Bang! Rumble! Flash! Ching!

Yeah it's over . . .
Now I've got a headache now.
        Bang! Still there.

Fred Hunt (10)
Ferrars Junior School

MY SANDWICH

My sandwich was pretty big you know,
I made it all myself,
Do you want to know all the ingredients?
Egg, sausage, cucumber, carrots, baked beans,
Tomato soup, yoghurt, crisps, chocolate bar, orange.
My sandwich was pretty nice you know.

After that I made my sister one,
She ate it and we were taking it in turns to go to
                                        the bathroom.
And you can guess what for.
My mum came in from work and said,
'Anyone hungry? I'm starving.'

Michelle McCabe (9)
Ferrars Junior School

STARS

Stars twinkle and stay bright.
Stars go with the moon at night.
Stars make the sky bright and light.
Stars are there to wish on at any night.
Stars are there to keep you safe.
Stars are playing when you can't see.
Stars come out to help you see.
Stars make pictures that you can see.
One of the stars is your special star.
Stars are playful, happy and joyful.
Five is my lucky number, just like a star.
Stars come out to play.
Stars are there so you can say a secret.

Jemma Oatley (9)
Ferrars Junior School

CHRISTMAS DAY

I woke up on Christmas Day,
I ran downstairs and shouted '*Hooray*!'
I look up at the tree and gazed,
And before I knew it I was in a daze.
When I shook the box to guess what's inside,
I thought to myself 'Shall I share?' I had to decide.
When I looked at all my toys,
I jumped up and down and made a loud noise.

Dharana Patel (11)
Ferrars Junior School

LOVE POEM

Your smile is as bright as the yellow sun.
Your eyes twinkle like the stars in the night sky.
Your hair feels like silk when I run my hand through
it.
Your lips feel like smooth cotton wool.
Your skin is as soft as velvet.
You are the one for me.

Perry Gullifer (11)
Ferrars Junior School

THE STARS

The shooting stars are running across the sky.
The diamonds are twinkling in the moonlight.
The stars flash as they come to life.
The stars get brighter and brighter as they come to us.

Becki-Jo Bull (9)
Ferrars Junior School

THE WEATHER

Lightning is a sparkler in the sky
It's lit by Mother Nature.
For everyone to enjoy.

The stars are little diamonds in the sky
They shine over you from above.

Snow is soft, it's also cushions.
It's cold and wet
It's white and dirty.

Alisha Oakley (9)
Ferrars Junior School

THE STARS

The stars are diamonds in the moonlit sky.
You want to reach up, but they're too high to reach,
glittering, glowing in the dark.
In space no one knows how high or low
                              the stars are.
But the stars are always diamonds in the dark black
                                        night.

Faye Clarke (10)
Ferrars Junior School

CLOUDS OF CANDY FLOSS

Clouds are candy floss
lovely and sweet floating in the air.
I just want to grab it and eat it.
It's just floating in the air.

Steven Redmond (10)
Ferrars Junior School

THE WOODLAND ROBIN

I'm a robin hopping along,
Listen and you'll hear my song.
Look up high and you'll see me fly,
Way up there in the bright blue sky.

I'm a robin friendly and true,
Here in the garden just like you.
Watch me on the cold winter days,
See me still in the summer blaze.

Remember me now as you grow tall,
Perched on top of your garden wall.
I'm the robin with the bright red breast,
The woodland bird that you love best.

Adam Meade (11)
Ferrars Junior School

RAIN

It's a dragon,
It lashes about,
hitting against the rooftops of my house,
and it bashes,
and it lashes,
as it hits the ground.

Now it's blocks of ice
hitting against my window.

I daren't get out of bed,
who knows what
might happen . . .?

Stacey Adams (10)
Ferrars Junior School

I'M A BIG FAT BUDGIE

I'm a big fat Budgie.
I don't do a lot.
Might park on my perch,
Might peck in my pot,
Might peek in my mirror,
Might ring my bell,
Might peer through the bars of my fat
budgie cells.
Might say 'Who's a pretty boy then?'
Might not.
I'm a big fat budgie.
I don't do a lot.

Safiyah Malik (11)
Ferrars Junior School

THE MYSTERY OF LOVE

I'm in love with a guy
called David,
Is he in love with me?
If love would just grow on trees.
Where would we be?
Sometimes I wonder
if we could be history.
My best friend Christy says
it's not meant to be,
But I know it's going
Perfectly.

Latanya Bailey (10)
Ferrars Junior School

SNOW

The snow comes down as feathers.
Cotton wool as well.
It comes down from them candyfloss clouds.
That are drifting through the sky.

The sky which is floating and drifting.
And the clouds which let out the snow.
That drifts in the sky.
And when you look up, the sky looks like an iceberg.

Michael Blanchard (10)
Ferrars Junior School

THE STARS

The stars are twinkle diamonds that are in the sky.
They shine so bright they make the sky light up.
If you gaze up at them they gaze at you back,
                                    with a smile.
They twinkle as crystals in the sky,
they blast with silent dreams.

Lauren Oakley (9)
Ferrars Junior School

THUNDER

Thunder is rocks falling from the mountains
Rumbling in the sky
It is a devil shouting very loudly
A giant stomping its feet like
Sixteen hammers dropped on the floor.

Chrystal Daley (9)
Ferrars Junior School

SHERBET LEMONS

When I take a piece of sherbet lemon and put it in my mouth,
It's so fizzy, I think that I've swallowed a firework.

I don't care, if it is wet or cold,
I just suck and suck my sherbet lemon until I explode.

I can't eat another yet, but maybe at six, but at seven I
felt sick.

Jamie Gales (9)
Ferrars Junior School

SHERBET LEMONS

When I take a sherbet lemon it tastes
like a volcano erupting in my mouth.
And I suck and suck until the sherbet comes out.
It's like a fizzy ball melting in my mouth.
It was popping in there.
Then it was gone.

Robin Dowling (9)
Ferrars Junior School

I SAW

I saw an elephant swimming in the lake,
I saw a snake eating the moon,
I saw a hippo eating a zebra,
I saw a lion going to the wizard,
I saw a tiger flying in the sky.

Stuart Glenister (9)
Ferrars Junior School

THE WITCH'S SPELL

Frog's legs, bat's ears,
Cat's blood, snail's tear,
Chicken's wings, human's liver,
Enough to make you shiver.

Pig's bones, rat's nose,
Lizard's veins, bear's paws,
Dragon's teeth, hog's tail,
Worm's maw, fish scales
Disgusting!

Bobble, bobble, mix about
Stir it fast or I'll
Shout!

Kayleigh McDevitt (9)
Ferrars Junior School

A SILLY POEM

Crazy shoes,
Parents drinking booze!
Little frogs,
Tail-wagging dogs!
Elephants eating!
A witches spell,
A little boy's head and cat's tail!
Green grass -
White grass -
Red grass -
Blue grass -
Little heads
And a big bed.

James-Anthony Burroughs (10)
Ferrars Junior School

MICE

I like nice mice.

With their little pink tails
Their grey claws
And great marble-eyes.
They run along the floor
No one ever sees them
Because they're so fast.

They have great white teeth.
And eat lots of cheese.
I don't know why
People don't like mice.

I like nice mice.

Katrina Russell (9)
Ferrars Junior School

DONUTS

Some are squishy
Some are fat
Some are gooey
Which make you fat.

Some are empty
Some are puffed
Some are lovely
With jam stuffed.

Some are big
Some are small
I think that I can
Eat them all!

Zeeshan Sheikh (11)
Ferrars Junior School

SHERBET LEMON

They fizz!
They bubble!
You suck!
You crunch!
They let out this lovely taste!
They let you suck the sherbet out!
You can taste the lovely sherbet!
You can taste the tangy lemon!
They let it all out then it gets smaller!
They make it so small you nearly swallow it!
You give it one last suck!
You give it a final crunch and it turns into a
                              blown up asteroid!
And finally it's gone!

Martin Daniels (9)
Ferrars Junior School

THUNDER AND LIGHTNING

The clouds grow dark
And thunder comes to
Destroy the city.
Here comes lightning to
Help thunder destroy the city.
With those zig-zags.
Yellow daggers destroying the city,
No one knows what happened next . . .

Zaed Parkar (9)
Ferrars Junior School

SAT TEST

The school bell rings
It's time for our test,
This horrible feeling
It takes powerful stress.
It's all about science
It makes my head turn,
I can't do this question,
I don't want to learn.
The time is up,
I haven't written a thing
Just wait till my mum gives a slap
                    on my chin.
Tomorrow is here,
And the bell rings again,
Another test, I'm turning insane!

Leon Moore (10)
Ferrars Junior School

THUNDER AND LIGHTNING

The lightning is a giant devil pushing
his golden fork into the ground.
Thunder joins him with an explosion
Sound - Bang, crash, boom pound.

Another flash of forked lightning
Zig zagged across the sky as if the sky
                    was being *electrocuted.*
Thunder moaned and groaned as sheets of hail hit
                                the ground.

Peter Winters (10)
Ferrars Junior School

THINKING ABOUT VALENTINE'S DAY

Since I was five,
Every Valentine's day,
I received gifts,
Not February but May!

The gifts I had,
Were from dorks or geeks,
But a couple of times,
They were from freaks.

This year's Valentine's day,
I would like a gift,
From someone who will hold me,
When I'm scared on a lift.

Someone wonderfully-glorious,
So magically-kind,
Magnificently-Fascinating,
I wish someone like that I could find!

But what if this isn't true,
The boy I think of might not be,
Though I think I'm true,
That somewhere . . . someone . . . is there for me!

Moriom Begum (10)
Ferrars Junior School

THE THINGS ABOVE

The sky is a fluffy blue blanket,
Rolling in your bed.
The sky is a sweet blue ice lolly,
Dripping on your head.

Thunder crashes and lashes on the ground,
It is your enemy.
Thunder is a big red devil,
Waving his deep sharp knife.

Seonad O'Donoghue (9)
Ferrars Junior School

QUEEN VICTORIA IS WAITING

Queen Victoria was waiting
Her artist is creating
The prince was going to dine
His son was learning to mime
The guards are playing charades
The princess is escaping.

Why oh why did she leave
Is it because I told her about Adam and Eve?
Oh me lady
She'll come back.

So Queen Victoria was waiting and waiting
Then after that the princess married a bat
When the queen saw the paper she lost her temper
The chap turned out to be the prince of Cuba.

When they came back the queen gave a ceremony
The town was roaring but the guards were snoring.
From there on the queen was never kept waiting again.

Only 100 more times!

Thomas Evans (10)
Ferrars Junior School

LOOKING FOR A FRIEND

I'm looking for a good friend
I'm looking for a great friend
I'm looking for a best friend
               in the world.
He must like football,
He must like singing
someone just like me who's free like me.
And enjoys playing with me.
Who likes to be free with me.
The best friend in the world
Who wants to play with me.

Ashley Bateman (9)
Ferrars Junior School

SPIDERS

Spiders, spiders, everywhere.
One on the floor and one on the stair.
One in your room,
And one in your hair.
Spiders, spiders, everywhere.
Spiders on your bedroom door
bouncing about from floor to floor.
Spiders crawling through little holes
and maybe in the bath plug hole.
I may sound horrible but they can't hurt you,
               or can they?

Kirsty Garner (9)
Ferrars Junior School

SHERBET LEMONS

When I eat a sherbet lemon,
It is extremely fizzy,
With all of the juice
Popping in my mouth.

I don't care which flavour I have,
I just like the fizzing,
Like a volcano exploding with juice.

It is as sweet as some chocolate
With a different flavour to it.
Sherbet lemons are very, very sweet
With its fizzing taste.

But as I suck it
It slowly disappears.

Simon Long (8)
Ferrars Junior School

SHERBET LEMONS

When I take
A piece of sherbet lemon
It's like a firework
Bursting in my mouth.

I don't care
Where I am
As long as I have got my sherbet
Exploding in my mouth.
Suddenly what has happened?
It's disappeared.

Holly Wingrave (9)
Ferrars Junior School

A WITCH'S CAULDRON

Here are a few things you might find in a witch's cauldron.
A pair of flies and four newt eyes.
A camels hump and a fist that can thump.
A reindeer horn and a snake that has just been born,
and a raging storm.
A polar bear for a cat's purr.
A tiger's roar and a giant door.
Ten frogs' legs and three pirates on pegs.
Sixteen bat wings.
Lots of dark and evil things.
So don't go near to a big old cauldron,
or you'll be part of the stew!

Niall Bingham (9)
Ferrars Junior School

THE MONSTERS

They live in my house,
They even ate my mouse,
I tried to get them out,
but they all know how to shout.
Their singing drives me mad,
I'm getting out of hand,
the family don't know what to do,
I would love to see them go.
They sleep in the shed without a bed!
We try to get away
but they all want us to stay.
We said we would make them a pie,
instead they all said goodbye!

Thomas Smith (10)
Ferrars Junior School

MY DOG

Dogs are tender and loving
they are soft, fluffy and comfy
they care for you
if you care for them too.
They might hug, touch and give you their
                                        paw
they might even sleep on you and snore.
But that's dogs and you can't stop them
You run you jog but you still can't catch up
they eat drink and sleep a lot too.
But guess what? I don't care
Cause it's my dog and that ends there.
My dog's name is Destiny and she's a nice dog
and really fast too.
You know what.
I said to her one day I can't catch up with you.
I really can't. I wish I had four legs like you.
So I can catch up with you so I don't run out of
                                        breath.
Anyway I don't care cause
I think she's the best.

Lorine Barker (10)
Ferrars Junior School

SHERBET LEMON

I look at my sherbet lemon,
I say 'sherbet lemon, sherbet lemon'
Fizzy, cracking
Sherbet lemon.
It is like a volcano in my mouth.
And a strawberry on a summer's day.

Louise Waller (9)
Ferrars Junior School

BABIES

Babies scream
Babies cry
Babies stay up every night
Give them a bottle
Let them toddle.

They may need a new nappy
But don't be unhappy
Just change their nappy
And be happy.

You may be tired
But then just get rewired
Because you are not supposed to be
tired if you've got a baby.

Give them a kiss and a good wish
Then they will be asleep like a treat.

Asha Edwards (10)
Ferrars Junior School

I SAW . . .

I saw a tiger drinking all the water.
I saw a bird with one foot.
I saw a fly hopping on two feet.
I saw a kangaroo fly in the sky.
I saw a rabbit saying he's deaf.
I saw a crocodile being a helicopter.
I saw a lady jumping around.
I saw a man doing shopping around and
                                about.

Lewis Downing (9)
Ferrars Junior School

SHERBET LEMONS

When I saw the sherbet lemon and put it in my mouth,
it was so tasty all the juice came out.

I don't care what time of day
I can't resist my sherbet lemon
It was so lovely I shouted hooray.

It's like fireworks popping in my mouth.

It went down and popped,

Can't wait till tomorrow what will happen next . . .

Dean Wrench (9)
Ferrars Junior School

SPACE

Once I was in space
When I had a race.
And I found a friend
Who had a cat.
Who had gone missing
And I said listen.
Let's get a dog
Let's go on an expedition.
And go and get your cat.
I hope it's still alive.

Shaye McFadden (9)
Ferrars Junior School

THERE'S A MONSTER DOWNSTAIRS

I creep downstairs I creep and creep
to watch TV. I put it on and I sit down.
Some one hugs me
I think it's dad
I go to sleep.
He puts me to bed
My eye opens,
it's a monster.
He giggles and giggles.
I run to wake up mum and dad.
They go downstairs to see what's there.
Nothing there so let me close my ears.
I close my eyes and squeeze my feet.
I wake up in the morning
to have my breakfast.
The monster ate my breakfast.
And ate ice cream.
Oh Dear Oh Dear
What Comes Next?

Mahwish Abbas (10)
Ferrars Junior School

HICKORY DICKORY DOCKING

Hickory Dickory Docking
The mouse went in the
stocking
It smelt like cheese
The mouse had fleas
It really was quite
shocking.

Cara Edwards (11)
Ferrars Junior School

SHERBET LEMON

When I eat a Sherbet Lemon,
It feels really fizzy,
It makes me dance and makes me dizzy,
It makes me explode when I eat one,
It's even better than a chocolate bun.

It's like a volcano bursting and bubbling
Then I start chuckling,
But when it's over,
The fizzy, dizzy, exploding,
Sherbet Lemon is over.

I eat and eat and eat again,
The end.

Felicity Price (8)
Ferrars Junior School

I SAW

I saw a bird dancing the jive,
I saw a panda making a magic spell.
I saw an iguana hopping away.
I saw a snail snapping its jaws.
I saw a cat running up the tree.
I saw a pencil case watching me.
I saw a kangaroo wagging its tail.

Nicki Clark (9)
Ferrars Junior School

WEATHER

What is a hailstones?
- A cloud broken up.

What makes snow white?
- A big bucket of white paint.

What is fog?
- Steam out of a boiled kettle.

Why is snow cold?
- Because it got put in the freezer.

What is the sun?
- A big bright light bulb.

What is rain?
- The clouds when they cry.

David Bliss-McGrath (10)
Foxdell Junior School

TOUGH DOG

A great dribbler,
A ball sport,
A wild chaser,
A terrific guard,
A terrifying bark,
Large sharp claws,
Mega pointy teeth,
A nasty growl.

Kay Lerpiniere (10)
Foxdell Junior School

WHAT IS . . .

Why does it rain?
So the giant's garden grows.

How does it rain?
With a giant watering can.

How does the sun shine?
With a flashing torch.

Why is the sun hot?
Because the dragons ate chilli.

What is fog?
The smoke from a chimney.

How does the wind blow?
With a hairdryer.

Where does the wind go?
To put out a fire.

Bed Now!

Taja Balu-Smith (11)
Foxdell Junior School

MY SISTER CHARLOTTE

She's a stroppy so and so,
A sweet girl,
An argumentative person,
A daydreamer,
A grown up girl.
But most of all
She's a loveable sister.

Eloise Wilkin (10)
Foxdell Junior School

What Is?

Why is the sun hot?
Because an astronaut lit a match.

Where does rain come from?
A giant melted his ice lolly.

What is lightning?
A giant taking a picture of his family.

What is an Earthquake?
A giant jumping into an ocean.

What is thunder?
A giant falling off a cliff.

What is . . .
I don't know, go away!

Junaid Mughal (10)
Foxdell Junior School

What Is It?

A Big roarer
A Tree climber
A Fruit eater
A Fast runner
A Quick getaway
A Great carer
A Good fighter.
          It's a Gorilla.

Callum Murnane (10)
Foxdell Junior School

THE WEATHER

What is a tornado?
- A drill digging into the ground.

What makes the sun glow?
- A giant left his torch on.

What are hailstones?
- Stones falling from heaven.

What is fog?
- A giant's car exhaust fumes.

What is thunder?
- The Gods getting angry.

What is ice?
- Leave me alone!

What is a puddle?
Go to Bed!

Ohhhhhh!

Christopher McPhee (10)
Foxdell Junior School

MY PARROT

My parrot is funny.
It eats sunflower seeds.
It is grey and red,
It talks and goes on my mum.
I like my parrot, but sometimes
My parrot bites people!

Roy Goodhew (10)
Foxdell Junior School

WEATHER OR NOT

Why is the snow cold?
-Someone threw it out of the freezer.

What is thunder?
-It's just the giant running after Jack.

Why is the sun hot?
-God left it too long in the oven

Why is the rain wet?
-It came out of the bath without drying itself.

What is the thunder storm?
-The ten ladies dancing.

What is snow?
-Go to bed for Heaven's Sake!

Anam Sajjad (10)
Foxdell Junior School

IN THE WINTER

In the winter, at dawn,
There's always frost on the lawn.

In the winter, at noon,
It gets dark very soon.

In the winter, at night,
You might get frost bite.

Matthew Day (11)
Foxdell Junior School

WHAT IS WEATHER?

What is fog?
Someone's smelly breath.

Why is it raining?
A giant wet the bed.

Why is it not sunny?
The sun took a holiday.

What is snow?
The sky is falling.

Who is Jack Frost?
A ghost from the past.

David Lovell (112)
Foxdell Junior School

THE WEATHER

What is rain?
A giant crying.

What is lightning?
A flash of a camera.

What is a puddle?
An insect'swimming pool.

What is the sun?
A glowing coin tossed in the air.

What is . . .
Go To Bed!

Kevin Francis (11)
Foxdell Junior School

THE MAGIC BOX

I will put in the box
the witches black cat
the soul of the dragon
and the magical spells of the witch.

I will put in the box
a tiger's sharp teeth from his glittery
                              mouth.
A cheetah's eye like a shining star.

I will put in the box
a sharp nail from a dinosaur's claw
an angry dragon breathing out fire.

My box is designed with crystal and diamond,
the top is as shiny as a star
covered with spiky chains.

I will bury it under the ground in the back yard,
             so no one can steal it.

Usama Saleh (9)
Foxdell Junior School

A CHEETAH

A lightning speed,
A smooth turner,
A silent predator,
A fussy eater,
A valuable hunter,
An instinctive smeller,
A furry kitten,
A giant pack.

Hussnain Mohyuaoin (11)
Foxdell Junior School

THE MAGIC BOX

I will put in the box
An island with secrets of hidden treasure
A gold cave with hidden treasure and only
my friends are allowed and me.
A magic lamp that can give lots of wishes.

I will put in the box
Harry Potter to help me with my homework.
I will get a dragon to beat Ben up.
I will have my friends in the box.

My box is made of
Glittering stars dazzling of gold,
It is a star shape,
Inside it is a soft silk.

I will put it
In the Atlantic Ocean at the bottom of the sea.

Kasam Khan (10)
Foxdell Junior School

MY BEST FRIEND

We'll be friends forever,
Even when we're not together.
You're so cute and tiny,
But thank heavens your not whiney.
Even though you're only three,
You're my best friend as everyone can see.
We'll be friends forever,
Even when we're not together.
Always.

Mariessa Joseph (11)
Foxdell Junior School

THE MAGIC BOX

I will put in my box
a sparkly star in the sky at night
beautiful flowers growing in the garden
sun shining in the sky to make the flowers grow.

I will put in my box
a posh fairy
a cuddly teddy bear
a pretty rose that smells sweet.

I will put in my box
a wiggly pencil
a shaking ruler
a jumping rubber
it is a book that stays still.

I will lock my box with a shiny key
and I will hide it under my bed.

Raqia Shah (9)
Foxdell Junior School

A VIEW OF A RAT

A disease giver
A garbage eater
A stylish jumper
A nasty biter.
A sneaky arriver.
A raisin dropper.
A tail snapper.
A fierce looker.

Danny Goodall (11)
Foxdell Junior School

THE MAGIC BOX

I will put in the box
A doll who was beautiful
A seven ball on the floor
Tom and Jerry running.

I will put in the box
A witch who is nasty
A monkey who is jumping around.
The fairy in the water.

I will put in the box
Me sitting on my chair
Me reading a book
Me playing with the computer.

My box is made of rubber.

I will put it in a beautiful jungle.

Jason Cosby (9)
Foxdell Junior School

A VIEW OF A MOBILE PHONE

A swift dialler,
A game player,
A fashion shower,
A message sender,
A stylish cover,
A phone number storer,
A wicked communicator,
A portable mover.

Ashley Messer (11)
Foxdell Junior School

MY MAGIC BOX

I will put in my box.
The philosopher's stone from Harry Potter.
A girl who sells magic stones.
All my scaletric so I can magically beat Danielle.

I will put in my box
The badly beaten Danielle
The winning race car,
The shining gold cup and race car.

My box is made of
Glittering glistening yellow stars and
crescent moons for hinges.

I will bury it on an island in Jamaica in the hot
blazing sun.

Leon Gillard (10)
Foxdell Junior School

GRASSHOPPER

Jim the grasshopper is ten feet tall,
He always goes round playing with a ball,
He's really big and fat,
And sleeps in a cow pat,
Lives in a barn,
Where no-one can harm,
His scales are twelve feet wide,
And they all go slide,
His hair is 4.93 metres long,
And all day it goes boing, boing, boing.

Shelina Choudhury (10)
Foxdell Junior School

BEWARE OF THE JELLYMAN!

Beware of the jellyman,
He's coming for you,
He'll find you no matter what you do!

Beware of the jellyman,
You'll be crushed like a can,
And turned into a pan!

Beware!

Now you know what he does . . .
Look behind you,
Boo!

Bianca Moncrieffe (10)
Foxdell Junior School

A FOOTBALLER'S DREAM

When I was young,
I wanted to be a footballer,
and play for Brazil.
Wear the best yellow kit,
and strike a goal in the net.
Oh Ronaldo see a little boy
Cheering for you.
And take me with you when you
play next time for Brazil.

Adeel Hussain (8)
Foxdell Junior School

NIGHT

He makes me scared all night,
It's night he's old and tall,
Creeps mysteriously with his big black cloak,
Covering half of the world,
His eyes are big and wide,
He has got a mysterious face,
That I can't work out.
He's always quiet and moves silently,
He's a spooky person that plays tricks,
In the dark he makes me feel like I'm blind,
He gives me nightmares,
He lives in a dark tall house.

Shafaq Rathore (11)
Foxdell Junior School

MY MUM

She's a warm, soft, comfortable bed,
An energetic Jamaican.
She's a poisonous snake,
An eagle gliding in the sky.
She's a golden sunflower in the sun.
A lovely beautiful whistling sound,
She's a glittering starry night.
A fizzy tango with lots of happiness,
She's a detective, she knows everything.
She's a juicy pizza ready to be eaten.
She's a warm sweater to be hugged.

Nile Lovindeer (9)
Foxdell Junior School

THE MAGIC BOX

I will put in the box
The Rock the bramen bull
A Harry Potter book
Ben Evans the history genius.

I will put in the box
A big fat dictionary filled with candy
A round shaped rabbit
A slimy, mouldy hat.

My box is made of
Brown silky material
A leather feel to the outside.

I will put it in a bank safe
where nobody can touch it.

Jerry Gibbons (9)
Foxdell Junior School

MY MUM

She's a rocking chair,
She's a glamorous ballroom,
She's a fluffy rabbit,
She's a flying pigeon,
She's a pink blossom,
Sometimes a screeching monkey,
A twinkling night,
Forever red wine,
An organised business woman,
A scrumptious feast,
A glittering dress.

Liz Fletcher (9)
Foxdell Junior School

Happy Christmas!

It was Christmas Eve,
I had to leave food for Santa
I couldn't get to sleep
Finally Christmas Day came.
I like to tear the paper back,
They came from Santa's black sack,
When I've opened all my presents
My mum bought in two more
As I dug I saw a great big box
And knew it wasn't socks,
As I tore the paper off,
I saw a
PC
I love my mummy.
I played with my bop it
Mum said 'Stop it'
Friends and family had a feast,
Potatoes, chicken, turkey and pudding.
Didn't go to bed till morning.

Shannen Pardy (9)
Foxdell Junior School

I See An Angel

Christmas holly hanging down
Snowing gently on the ground.
Reindeer's bells are on the roof.
Santa's footprint in the room.
Elves are working hard and strong.
Angels singing all day long.
I made a wish on a star, can you guess
                    what I asked for?

Darryl McKay (9)
Foxdell Junior School

LENNOX LEWIS

He's a rough strong brick.
He's a metal table worth millions.
He's a fierce dangerous looking lion with red eyes.
He's a black and red flying bat.
The smell of a gumshield.
He's a heavyweight Champion.
He's the best boxer.

Mehran Khan (9)
Foxdell Junior School

MIKE TYSON

He's an angry cooker.
He is a thick wall.
He is a black panther.
The smell of a dirty pig.
The sound of danger.
The long thundering night.
A coke drink.
A strong boxer.

Farhaan Asad (9)
Foxdell Junior School

MY WISH

When I was younger,
I wished I was a super star,
Sparkling in the wind,
I saw a little star.
Hoping that I would make it,
Looking at the star.

Danielle McPhee (8)
Foxdell Junior School

THE MAGIC BOX

I will put in the box
A fierce lion to keep it safe
My hamster for good memories
I will put food to eat.

I will put in the box
My friends to play with
I will put plants so I can breathe
I will put books to read.

I will put in the box
A genius school
A long boat
The hot sun.

I will put in the box
I will put buildings
My sparky teacher
I will put shops.

My box is
Hard with gold in the corners
The top is shooting stars
Covered with black magic.
I will put it in the sea with me.

Jamie Gray (9)
Foxdell Junior School

MY DREAM NEVER CAME TRUE

When I was younger
I wished that my house
Was made out of chocolate
and sweets because I love
Chocolate and sweets.

But now I wished to
be a nurse or a doctor
to take care of people's
babies especially because
my auntie's baby
passed away.

Rabia Saghir (8)
Foxdell Junior School

JAMES BOND

He's a secret bookcase hiding in a secret passage.
He's a transparent bedroom window.
He's a ghost of a powerful Egyptian cobra.
A kestrel sitting on its post eyeing his prey.
A soft sound of light footprints and a thumping heart.
An interesting night full of fireworks and danger.
A stirred martini
A secret agent.

Abbas Ali (9)
Foxdell Junior School

MOVING THINGS

A car zooming on the road,
An aeroplane flying in the sky
The thunderous lorry crossing the bridge.

A tiger creeping through the forest,
A man's horse galloping on the field.
An elephant stomping in the jungle.

Shohidur Rahman (9)
Foxdell Junior School

THE MAGIC BOX

I will put in my box
The seven golden dragons.
The sparkling ten diamonds.
All my golden medals.

I will put in my box.
All my golden necklaces.
And my books of fairy tales.

My box is made of
Gold outside.
Silk and cotton inside.
And diamonds in the corners.

I will bury it
in the ancient Egyptian tomb.

Imran Tariq (10)
Foxdell Junior School

MEMORIES

The best day ever;
Remembering my ninth birthday,
Waking immediately,
I smell hot food cooking.
Remembering three presents wrapped,
In shiny silver sparkly paper,
I felt these three hard boxes,
Before opening them.
I heard my family singing Happy Birthday
My step-dad gave me a drink of Coca-cola,
The best day ever.

Simone Robinson (9)
Foxdell Junior School

THE MAGIC BOX

I will put in my box
A shiny globe going very fat,
A sun soft walk around.
The Earth spinning around.

I will put in my box
A lion roaring like a sheep,
A tiger growling like a dog
A dog wuffing like a tiger.

My box is made of
wood as shiny seed.
I will put my box in the soil.

Maryam Bibi (9)
Foxdell Junior School

WISH POEM

When I was younger,
I wished I was a policeman,
wearing nice smart clothes,
and a police badge that glows.

Arresting people, helping people,
Driving big fast cars,
putting bad people
behind big black bars.

Now I wish I could be a taxi driver,
Just like my dad,
Driving people around and
Charging them one pound.

Ateeq Choudhury (8)
Foxdell Junior School

CHRISTMAS SPIRIT

On Christmas morning
I wake up at four o'clock
I open my presents with glee,
I got a scooter
a ring
and lots more.

My Auntie came round.
She fainted on the ground when Don
proposed to her.
That made her day.
And then I heard her say
Yes
To celebrate we had turkey,
roast potatoes, stuffing,
sausages, ice-cream.
It was yummy.

All day I rode my scooter,
and wore my ring.

I had lots of fun on
Christmas day.
I wish it could be Christmas
every day.

Jessica Hunter (8)
Foxdell Junior School

THE BOGEY MAN

In the darkest damp cave,
Lurks the creepy crawly bogey man
His face is dark and gloomy and gungy
And gory he eats lovely, lonely children
Bones crushed and crumpled lying all
over the place.

Sameena Shakur (10)
Foxdell Junior School

IN THE SUMMER

In the summer it's hot
No rain, no rainbows, not even a gold pot
Holidays, having fun
What's that shining? The sun!

In the summer it's cool
Because there's no more school
Children eating ice-cream
Everything has a coat of green

In the summer the children playing
All the animals sleepily laying
Holidays, having fun
What's that shining? The sun!

Bhipashah Yasmin (10)
Pirton Hill Junior School

THE CHASE

Oh my goodness who's that, who's there?
I hope it's not a Polar bear.
What's that over there, who's following me?
It best not be a bumble bee.
Come on, own up, stop being so rough,
I'm tired of you, I've had enough.
Just go away. Who are you? A spy?
Be quiet, shut up or it's your eye.
Go away, you, or I'll tell my mother,
Fine. 'Click' goes the light.
Oh, it's just my brother.

Sharelle Bailey (11)
Pirton Hill Junior School

UNDER THE SEA, I GO

Under the sea, I go
To a magical underwater world,
With -
Fish
Jellyfish
Octopus with legs
Sharks
Seals
And other things.
Under the sea, I go
To a magical underwater world.

Renate O'Connor (10)
Pirton Hill Junior School

SUMMER

The sun is shining, the clouds are moving.
The kids are out, the parents bathing.
The swimming pools are out,
With water spilling.

Parents with barbecues and friends.
Kids with squirt guns on targets.
The barbecue is hot with burgers.
The children are getting better.

The jumping board is cool.
The kids are splashing around in the pool.
The parents are coming,
The kids are loading then . . .
Splash!
Whoosh!
The parents are wet for good.

Paul Young (9)
Pirton Hill Junior School

CHRISTMAS TIME

Christmas time is lots of fun,
Lots of fun for Everyone.
See them dance and shout and sing,
It's Christmas time again.
Yummy mince pies on the table,
Eating and watching the cable.
Everybody has fun and eats turkey too,
The holiday has finished now,
What a lovely day - *Phew!*

Latifah Cain-Greaves (8)
Pirton Hill Junior School

SUMMER

Summer is hot, a day
to go to the beach.
When you wake up in the morning
the sun shines in your eyes.

Children get headaches and
go crying to their mums.
The sun goes really yellow
like a football made out of fire.

People have water fights
and get soaking wet.
Sometimes a little boy gets in the way
and gets squirted in his face.

Nico Gonsalves (9)
Pirton Hill Junior School

SPRING

Spring-a-ding-a-ling
It's the marvellous day of spring
Flowers dance
Like rings that go round and round in a ring

Baby animals come out to play and eat
Like monsters that greet
Trees grow with brown coats
And the grass grows with green coats

Fruits grow tasty and yummy
Spring-a-ding-a-ling
Today's the saddest day of all because
It's the last day of spring

Sheraz Ahmed (9)
Pirton Hill Junior School

AUTUMN LEAVES AND NATURE

Green, yellow, red and orange are colours of leaves
In autumn there is a strong breeze
Leaves in autumn are flying like birds
Bark on trees are hard wrinkles

No animals get born
Orange is the colour of the lawn
Everything is cold, getting near to winter
Children wear their gloves and coats

No longer the grass is green
Children play conkers and knock each other out
Nice and brown are the spiky green shells
Conkers fall off conker trees

Rahbiya Chaudaury (9)
Pirton Hill Junior School

SPRING

In spring new leaves,
Grow on tall trees.
The flowers grow in,
All different colours.

Lots of parents do,
Their spring cleaning.
Spring balls of blossom,
Grow on tall trees.

Quite a few babies,
Are born in spring,
Because it is such
A lovely season.

Emily Goldney (9)
Pirton Hill Junior School

SPRING

Children playing with their kites
on a nice relaxing day
children getting ice-creams
but they don't want to pay

The king is always singing
like it sounds nice
but everyone in their minds
think he sounds like squeaky mice

Playing races on the grass
like Linford Christy
I like the air, my friends don't care
it's not that misty

Animal mothers giving birth
but the other people just
go ahead and surf
it's just happy people on the Earth

Ryan Derby (9)
Pirton Hill Junior School

SNOW

Snow, snow in the sky
Falling down the golden eye
Falling through all the views
So many queues in the snow

Getting cold, never bold
Children have raw hands
Throwing snowballs at each other
More than the snow

Falling down like crystals
In the sky
Still falling through the golden eye
Children are saying

Noses are red, faces are blue
Follow me and I'll throw a snowball at you
But the snow won't last
So play and play until lunch

Lian Connolly (9)
Pirton Hill Junior School

WINTER

The snow is falling out the sky,
Like little crystals
When the rain drops by.

When the cars go by,
The rain drops behind,
When the cars go,
The wind blows
And the birds
Fly to snuggle up in their nests.

The clouds are moving far behind,
When the cars don't move,
The snow is glittering like stars at night.

When the cars go by,
The rain drops behind,
When the wind blows
The birds snuggle up in their nests.

Rio Sreedharan (9)
Pirton Hill Junior School

SUMMER DAYS

Summer mornings have come
butterflies, bees, snails, birds tweeting
Dog and cat laying on the soft green grass
like a mat.

Shiny sun, shiny sun, please burn down on me.
Hot and sweaty children
eating delicious food.
Ants crawling around for food.

Sunny sun, shiny sun, please burn down on me.
Children playing lovely games.
People in pools, swimming around like fish,
flowers so colourful, I can see them in my room.

So shiny sun, shiny sun, please burn down on me.
Children burning, it's so hot,
my mum's brown, not white one bit.
So shiny sun, shiny sun, please burn down on me.

Hannah Hunt (10)
Pirton Hill Junior School

SAW IT IN A RAINBOW

I saw it in the rainbow, a rainbow, a rainbow
I saw it in the rainbow, lots of pretty colours
This rainbow I saw was in the city, dull and dim
But this rainbow I saw in the city lightened the place
So it looked like a hall of summer flowers
Everyone looked out of their towers
To see the city full of flowers.

Danielle Sullivan (10)
Pirton Hill Junior School

WINTER

Glittery ice on the cold grass
The snow is thick on the car windows
In bed, nice and warm, do not want to get out of bed
In the snow, freezing cold, people turn to ice.

Icicles hanging from my ears and the rooftops of houses all sizes.
Cars do not start and animals are not cold
Because you've fur.
Lots of ice on the roads
And bins are covered in snow
And the streets are eerie.

The park ponds are frozen up hard
And no ducks on the ponds.
The fishes are sleeping, the squirrels are eating nuts
And getting ready to go to bed.
All I ever see is snow on this day.

Kimberley Dunbar (9)
Pirton Hill Junior School

SUMMER

A baking beach that's always mild,
Cool ice cream that shivers in the sun,
Spicy sun that glows in the day,
Smart seagulls fly in the fresh blue air,
Shimmering paddling pool that cools people down,
Short shorts that come down to your knees,
A fancy swimming pool that makes you go blue,
Pretty shells that makes the beach a nice place,
Vicious crabs that walk round slowly,
Round sun hats that shade your burning eyes.

Jodi Roach (8)
Pirton Hill Junior School

WINTER

Shiny frost in the grass like glitter shining fast.
People with red fat shining noses.
Animals cold and frosty.
Quick! Quick! Get to your homes or you'll fall asleep on your way.
So look! Look! Rabbits hopping with lots of food.
Bears with their honey in their caves.
Birds flying fast with worms for their children.
So why are you not in bed?
Houses with snow on the window sparkling bright.
The sun hiding low in the sky like she's so shy.

Sitara Ahmed (10)
Pirton Hill Junior School

LET'S GO ABSEILING

Let's go abseiling, let's try something new,
I'm not scared, I'm not scared,
Off a railway bridge, 50 feet or two,
I can't do this, I can't do this,
Safety gear on and over the edge I go,
Don't look down, don't look down,
One step at a time, nice and slow,
I can do it, I can do it,
Only a little way to go then I'm on the ground,
That was fun, that was fun!
A new adventure I have found,
Can I go again? Can I go again?

Daniel Hynes (9)
Pirton Hill Junior School

SUMMER WARMINGS

The boiling sun high up in the sky burning slowly.
Low shorts dangling down your legs nicely.
Happy children playing in the sun gently.
Cool T-shirts making your arms get boiling quickly.
Fun swimming pool making you cool tiredly.
Blackish sunglasses protecting your eyes nice and safely.
Delicious fruit waiting to be eaten happily.
High up birds racing down gently.
Really wet sweat dripping from your head immediately.
Real nice drink warming you up nicely.

Stephen Avery (8)
Pirton Hill Junior School

A FROSTY WINTER

Creaky snow making people's feet smelly
Stopped snowmen prancing about
Freezing frost making people shiver badly
Woolly hats white when they're finished with clumsily
Fierce fires burning brightly
Fluffy jumpers doing their jobs nicely
Solid snowballs getting thrown fiercely
Pointed snowflakes floating cautiously
Calm cars passing through the snow desperately
Bumpy boots gripping into the ground

Nathan James (8)
Pirton Hill Junior School

WINTER

Snow, snow in the rain
Falling on the windowpane
Glittering shiny white
Slithering falling sight

Snow, snow everywhere
There is a snowy hungry bear
Snow is cold and frosty
It was cold and foggy

There were big snowy balls
You can't break the rules
But one day
You can find your way

But one day
You can go out to play
It is foggy
My cat is called Moggy

Kirsty Warren (10)
Pirton Hill Junior School

WINTER

Frost is not that clear,
and when you breathe it is
like smoke comes out of
your mouth, nice and big.

In winter you need to wrap up nice
and warm but I don't want to
go out and Christmas is
around. Nice people have nowhere to go.

Snow is like sparkling glitter in the
sky. Snowflakes, like clouds, watch the
gold shoot down like the river,
like people in the sky and flashing
traffic.

Shaneen Simmonds (9)
Pirton Hill Junior School

MY OLD BIKE

My old bike was so cool
The colours were red, blue and green
Until it got squashed at school
After that it fell in the stream.

My old bike had a bell
Which was rusty
And it had a black seat
But it was dusty!

My old bike was so big
It went super fast
It nearly ran over a pig
Lucky that was the last.

My old bike was so cool
That's all I can say
It never ran out of fuel
There it is in my garage every day!

Roshni Sagoo (10)
Pirton Hill Junior School

HOUSES

H ow we live in houses
O n one floor are rooms which are big
U p to you what you do
S ome houses are small and big
E xcept a flat which is so big and tall
S ome people do them up and sell them.

Daniel Davies (11)
Pirton Hill Junior School

SWEETS ARE . . .

S weets are
W onderful,
E legant and
E dible, they're
T asty and
S our and also quite nice.

Michael Reed (10)
Pirton Hill Junior School

ROSE

R oses are red
O pen the buds
S oft velvet petals
E veryone seeing red
S now falling like pillows on red

Leanna Atkinson (8)
Pirton Hill Junior School

THERE WAS AN OLD MAN FROM JAMAICA

There was an old man from Jamaica,
Who was a very good Baker,
He chopped up some pork,
With a knife and a fork,
And shoved it in the pie maker.

Keval Shah (11)
Pirton Hill Junior School

WINTER

Slushy snow making cars crash
Giant snowballs rapidly firing on faces
Frozen ice seriously breaking bones
Beautiful snowflakes falling slowly
Scruffy scarves keeping us warm
Runny rain hailing so hard.

Oliver Meaton (9)
Pirton Hill Junior School

CHILDREN SAY

Children say on a rainy day,
It's cold and windy to go out to play,
Dogs bark to go to the park,
But it's cold and wet and getting dark.

Alexander Guthrie (11)
Pirton Hill Junior School

OUR TEACHERS AT SCHOOL

Our teachers at school
Are very cool,
Funny, kind and gentle,
But if you go wrong,
It takes so long,
To unwind the mess,
So it's wise to do your best!

Miss Dixon is the sporty type,
She is fun and most definitely cool!

Mr Moore is the football type,
He is fun and most definitely cool!

Mrs Auger is the literacy type,
She is fun and most definitely cool!

Mrs Ryan and Mr Burgess are the music type,
They are fun and most definitely cool!

Bryony Weston-Coombs (9)
Pirton Hill Junior School

WEATHER

Whenever I see rainy weather,
It makes me feel very clever.

When I see the sun come out,
It makes me get up and shout.

When both the rain and sun come up,
A rainbow appears and it goes up and up.

Andrew Joseph (11)
Pirton Hill Junior School

A HORRIBLE DAY AT SCHOOL

My teacher at school said,
You clean the hall,

But I said that only I,
I'm a spy,

And the school dinners were full of worms,
And they really squirm,

When I get home,
I groan and groan,

For some ice cream,
And if I don't get it I really scream,

I am so happy when I go home from school,
and I get to relax in the pool,

I have a best friend called Nicola,
Who lives in a trash bin called Coca-Cola.

Joanne Bailey (8)
Pirton Hill Junior School

THE BEST TEACHER

The best teacher
Has been the best for five years
Considerate, great and funny
Like a bright cheerful sun
Like an extraordinary sea
It makes me feel happy and excited,
Like I'm on the moon
The Best Teacher
Reminds us that we should be kind to all teachers.

Stacey Deamer (10)
Pirton Hill Junior School

FOREVER FRIENDS

Friends stay together
Over here and over there
Round the world with all the people understanding
Everywhere
Value of
Education, total
Respect and lots of care.

Friends that play together
Realising that they should share
Is
Every giving
Not just getting
Do this gladly
Show you care Forever Friends.

Jayna Kirankumar Patel (9)
Pirton Hill Junior School

WITCHES

Magic
is tragic
a witch would say
spells and poisons every day.
The lazy black cat gets in the way,
the bats might bite you,
the rats might fight you.
That's what a witch would say.

Cameron Devall (10)
Pirton Hill Junior School

DARKNESS . . .

Darkness is like . . .
A pair of black polished shoes,
A black felt-tip running out,
Dark coke all gone.

Darkness makes us . . .
Sleepy,
Tired,
Frightened.

Darkness . . .
Street lights go on and light up the town,
Stars and moons come up to the sky,
The builders stop building houses.

Kayleigh Payne (9)
Pirton Hill Junior School

THE VOLCANO

The volcano
Lava flows when
The top explodes,
Frizzling, breathtaking and huge,
It's like a terrifying mountain,
It's like an explosive bomb.
I feel bewildered, amazed and amused,
Like a pan of peas going pop!
The volcano
Reminds us that things
Are dangerous but amazing.

Leonie Maynard (11)
Pirton Hill Junior School

DARKNESS

Darkness is like . . .
Darkness coming towards you
Soft black velvet

Darkness makes us . . .
Shut our eyes
Frightened and scared

Darkness makes . . .
Stars a light
The moon come shining out
Street lights shimmer on
Cars put on their bight lights
Rabbits cuddling up together

Rebecca Rowley (8)
Pirton Hill Junior School

A SQUARE

A square, a square,
it has four sides,
a square, a square,
it's so plain,
a square, a square,
it has right angles,
a square, a square
and that's a square.

Stefan Walls (10)
Pirton Hill Junior School

FANCY DRESS

I had a fancy dress party,
Lots of my friends were there,
Claire was a sunflower,
Rikesh was a bear,
Luke was a wizard,
Stacey was a witch,
Niall came as a monster,
(It was making him itch.)
Daniel dressed up as a robot,
Nicola came as a clown,
But I went as a princesS
      But
      my
        wig
           fell
               off.

Ami Black (10)
Pirton Hill Junior School

THE TIDAL WAVE

The tidal wave
Can wipe out beaches
Huge, violent, slicing
Horses riding on the top
Still mounting the Earth
It makes me feel so weak
Like a rabbit to a fox
The tidal wave
Reminds me of a blizzard.

Nathan Cosher (10)
Pirton Hill Junior School

POOR LITTLE JIMMY

There once was a boy called Jimmy
Who could not stop picking his nose.
He licked it, he picked it, he rolled it, he flicked it
Until one day his finger got stuck.

Poor little Jimmy pulled in vain
He pulled and pulled and pulled again.
He tried and tired and tried once more
Until one day he came to his end.

All of his friends came to see his death
Everyone cried, even Evil Auntie Beth.
A few years later a friend came by
And pulled his skeleton finger from his nose
And Jimmy magically arose.

His human form started to grow
Now Jimmy won't ever pick his nose.

Proverb: Many hands make light work

Nicolas John Garland (11) & Floyd Billingy
Pirton Hill Junior School

DOGS, DOGS, DOGS

Spotty dogs and dotty dogs, they all look the same.
But wrinkly dogs and crinkly dogs almost look insane.
Grotty dogs and potty dogs always get hooked by a crane.
While scatty dogs and fatty dogs usually get the blame!

Laura Day (10)
Pirton Hill Junior School

DARKNESS

Darkness feels like a hand across your face,
Darkness feels like a mucky dark mist,
Darkness feels like nothing's there.

Darkness makes badgers come out,
Darkness makes us sleep earlier,
Darkness makes us feel tired,
Darkness makes us feel curlier,
Darkness makes us nap through the night,
Darkness makes the pigs doze.

Darkness is like the bottom of a box,
Darkness is like a curtain being drawn across the sky,
Darkness is like black hair on ahead,
Darkness is like a blackberry on my bed,
Darkness is like sooty mist.

Jordan Brown (9)
Pirton Hill Junior School

DEEP, DEEP, DEEP UNDER THE BLUE SEA

Deep, deep, deep under the blue sea,
My mum says to me, 'Catch a fish for tea.'
I caught the fish and it said, 'Please don't eat me.'
I put the fish back and it had a huge belly full of jelly.
Then I said, 'It's not silly, it's smelly.'
A school of fish swam by and caught my eye,
A jellyfish stung me,
Oh dear, oh dear,
To my eye it brought a tear.

Aisling Maynard (8)
Pirton Hill Junior School

WINTRY SEASONS

It's been snowing overnight
It's made a carpet of white
Kids come out to play
In the winter's night

Lights are on trees lighting up
The town when people
Walking by say oh wow
Present under trees, children can't wait

Cars will not move
Snow has jammed engines so
People walking by have to
Walk in the icy white road

Michael Anderson (10)
Pirton Hill Junior School

WARM SUMMER DAYS

The burning sun blazing rapidly
        Rushing sand going slowly
The blue sky blowing calmly
The smooth wind moving softly
    Old people resting lightly
    Green trees burning brightly
    White ice-cream melting coldly
    Little children playing nicely
The gentle air resting clearly
Tiny fishes swimming smoothly

Cory Belony (8)
Pirton Hill Junior School

DARKNESS

Darkness is like
A dry piece of black chair
and a dirty, muddy jumper
a board which is like a lid on a pen
and a wallet made out of leather

Darkness makes
creatures hibernate in the dark
and makes people petrified

Darkness makes
us sleep like a dead person
and scared too.
It makes us want to go out at night.

Joanne Brown (9)
Pirton Hill Junior School

WINTER

Floating fine in this air,
slimy snow falling on earth safely,
speedy sledges skating down hill slowly,
wooden skies ready to move happily,
furry hats clean and sparkly,
comfortable gloves ready to play sensibly,
knitted jumpers incredibly warm,
frozen ice stuffing doors tightly,
lively snowballs ready to aim carefully,
puffy snowmen running quickly.

Asti-Anna O'Donnell (8)
Pirton Hill Junior School

WINTER DAYS

Lovely bed making me hot meaninglessly,
Swishy snowflakes falling on my nose.
Super snow doing its job,
Hot bath always there for me.
Frozen frost trying to break bones furiously,
Incredible ice slippery and sticking to the ground.
Glowing gloves leaving my hands feeling tingly,
Small scarves wrapped 'round my neck.
Horrible hats pulled on my head,
Warm coats keeps me together.
Big boots holding my feet,
Boiling fire hot and too hard to touch.

Georgina Horne (8)
Pirton Hill Junior School

THE EARTH

The lively Earth
The lively Earth
Every second it turns around the sun.
It's a sphere,
It's massive,
It's adventurous.
It's like a round shape that humans live in.
It's like a ball bounced up in the sky.
It makes me feel like I'm surrounded by strangers.
Like a lonely tree sitting in a forest.
The lively Earth.
We think that the Earth is very small, but
Look how many things are in it!

Sneha Shah ()11
Pirton Hill Junior School

WINTER WARNINGS

Slimy snow slipping on our heads amusingly
Frozen frost making jobs complicated easily
Annoying rain stopping us from doing things furiously
Slithery sleet shaking our feet dangerously

Crispy snowflakes tickling our noses peacefully
Squelchy wellingtons squashing the sleet bumpily
Warm scarves shivery in the mist spookily
Cosy coats covering our body amazingly
Comfortable hats pulled on tight carefully
Holy snowman getting melted humorously
Invincible snowballs damaging people horribly
Flaming fire keeping us warm hopefully

Reynard Elvin (9)
Pirton Hill Junior School

I CAN FIND IT

Walking through the dark room,
Footsteps you can hear.
Wait! It's coming from over there,
I can see it. *Oh no,* I've lost it.
The thing is back again,
Drooling from its mouth.
It has something inside its mouth.
What can it be?
A sound is coming from the creature,
A moaning sound.
He switched on the light and . . .
Oh Lucy, there you are and how did you
Get out of your cot?

Christina Garland (11)
Pirton Hill Junior School

DARKNESS

Darkness is like: The king's black shoes that have just been polished.
Jail like all the lights have just been turned off.
A black river that is running through the tunnels.
A black rubbish bin that has just been painted.
Like big bold writing that has been written with ink.

Darkness: Makes us feel dopey and tired.
Makes the animals go back in their houses.
Makes us cuddle up to our mummies.

Darkness: Makes us scream all night.
Makes us have nightmares at night.
Makes the animals sniff all night.

Katie Fairall (8)
Pirton Hill Junior School

WINTER

Winter day when the weather is cold
And the wind goes swash, swish, swash
And the people stay in bed
So they're nice and warm.

Children playing in the snow
Children throwing snowballs
And they're making men
And getting very cold.

Children dressed in woolly clothes
So they're nice and warm
So they're wrapped up nice and warm
Now they're all ready to play games in the snow.

Shanade Collins (10)
Pirton Hill Junior School

SAMANTHA STRAWBERRY

Samantha Strawberry
Was very ordinary
Also very good
Until one day
She started to play, play and play
She mopped the hallway floor
Until she heard the nice white door
She ran as quick as she can
And saw a man and lady with a posh suntan
On her sensitive arm
In the middle of her palm
Was a little baby kitten
With two pairs of nice knitted mittens
The big cat was at home
Playing with her chewy gnome
While the father was finding a snack in the kitchen
Most of the time he was itching ~ itching ~ *itching!*

Valerie Tella (9)
Pirton Hill Junior School

THE OCEAN

The ocean
The ocean was there before mankind came
Stunning, beautiful, huge
Like a diamond ring shining
Like a road never ending.
It makes me feel I'm the only one alive
Like a lonely fish swimming through the water.
The ocean
It makes me think of peace and being calm.

Sarah Connolly (11)
Pirton Hill Junior School

REMEMBER ME

Remember me as a star twinkling in the sky.
You will find me in the sky
From night to night
Day to day, don't cry
I am here all the way.

Matthew Cummins (11)
Pirton Hill Junior School

GRANDAD

I loved him,
He loves me.
I miss him,
He loves me.
I want him,
He loves me.
I care about him,
He loves me.
I want to see him again,
But I won't,
He loves me.

Louisa Hunt (10)
Pirton Hill Junior School

THEE WAS A LADY WHO SAID 'HUSH'

There was a lady who said 'hush'
because she was combing her hair with a brush.
Her hair was so neat
so she put it in a pleat
and that was the lady who said 'hush'.

Leanne Bourne (11)
Pirton Hill Junior School

SCHOOL

I think school is boring
because my teachers are always snoring.
The playground's falling apart
but I always talk to my friend Bart.
I'm always in the same classroom and
the caretaker doesn't have a broom.
I think school is boring.

Ben Wolfe (11)
Pirton Hill Junior School

RAGING SEAS

Hopping frogs,
Dashing dogs,
Leaping llamas,
Hungry hogs.
Buzzing bees
In swaying trees
Storms across the raging seas.

Keri Murphy (10)
Pirton Hill Junior School

HAVE YOU EVER?

Ever gone to the circus, clowns are dipped in glue.
Ever been to the forest, green and scary too.
Ever been in a shop, food and drink for you.
Ever gone to the moon, slow and dusty too.
Ever done all those things, of course I have, because
I'm you!

Gareth Wilson (11)
Pirton Hill Junior School

THE TRAIN

Faster than light,
Faster than fear,
It runs on the track,
Like a spear.

As hard as might,
As hard as steel,
It goes round,
Like some wheels.

As calm as badgers,
As calm as rocks,
It comes round,
Like clocks.

As long as a snake,
Longer than cars,
We were on the train,
On the way to Mars.

Siobhan Robins (9)
Pirton Hill Junior School

REMEMBER ME

'Remember me when I am dead;
Look up into the sky and
I will be there
And I am one of the stars
Shining in your eyes
So look at this to remember
Me.

Carol Russell (11)
Pirton Hill Junior School

CHILDREN SAY THE FUNNIEST THINGS

Eat your greens!
Why? Why? Why?
You'll grow tall!
Why? Why? Why?

Don't eat chocolate!
Why? Why? Why?
You'll get fat!
Why? Why? Why?

Get inside now!
Why? Why? Why?
You'll catch a cold!
Why? Why? Why?

Don't throw your clothes!
Why? Why? Why?
They're brand new!
Why? Why? Why?

Stop riding on the dog!
Why? Why? Why?
You'll squash him to death!
Why? Why? Why?

Don't jump on the beds!
Why? Why? Why?
You'll break the springs!
Why? Why? Why?

Get to bed now!
No I don't want to!
It's not fair!

Alannah Gray (10)
Pirton Hill Junior School

WINTER DAYS

Snow is falling from the sky
Crashing down like blocks of ice
The clouds look like bits of wool
While people watch the snowballs fall

All the plants are covered in snow
And all the animals have nowhere to go
Kids are playing snowball fights
Quickly because it is nearly night

Then the kids are going in
As the night goes dark and dim
All the children eat some popcorn
Then go to bed and are nice and warm

Melissa Hudson (9)
Pirton Hill Junior School

WINTER

Frozen frost freezing fearfully
slithery snowflakes floating down carefully
frying fireplace drying clothes warmly
smooth snow crunching grass noisily
arctic ice turning hard solidly
shiny sleet sliming from the sky slowly
red hot hats roasting heads rapidly
gloomy gloves glowing
silky scarves keeping necks warm quickly
wet wellingtons dripping off daringly

Shareen Lewis (8)
Pirton Hill Junior School

TEACHERS

Miss Paine is *so* kind!
She is as nice as rice.
She understands everything
Then you've got Miss Dixon
Who cares about anything
She is into sports
She can be *so* naughty!
Mrs Colver can be funny
She can be *so* kind!
Mr Moor is *so* funny
He is sarcastic!
He is a good English teacher.
Miss Tomkin used to be here
But she left, sadly.
Got married probably.
Mrs Ryan likes music
And has a good sense of humour.

Charlotte Batchelor (10)
Pirton Hill Junior School

MY DETENTION

My detention was boring
Everyone was yawning
I was a writing a song
I know I was very wrong
I had to run fast
Or I would be late for class
The teacher was about to moan
Luckily the bell went and I ran home

Oliver Thomson (11)
Pirton Hill Junior School

DARKNESS

Darkness is like . . .
Black velvet in a calm town,
With shadows walking by which makes you shiver with gore.
Being trapped in a black hole,
Like fresh air at night.

Darkness makes us shiver if we are terrified
And start to get goose bumps.

Darkness makes us vicious when we believe in the bogeyman
And ghosts at night time.

Ryan McNamee (9)
Pirton Hill Junior School

MAGNIFICENT MOUNTAIN

The magnificent mountain,
Has been there for thousands of years
Huge, old, mighty
Like a saviour
Like a guardian of the world
I feel small
Like an unknown person
The magnificent mountain
Reminds us of the beauty of nature.

Claire Rushby (11)
Pirton Hill Junior School

WINTER

Slushing snow drifting down from the sky,
Slithering ice making cars skid dangerously,
A scary snowman frightening children away viciously,
Massive snowballs bashing people round the head cruelly,
An itching hat making you scratch madly,
A boiling coat making you burn up frantically,
A warm scarf making you comfortable and cosy,
A shiny sledge making you want to go on it seriously,
Freezing frost decorating the window beautifully,
Dropping rain falling fast from the sky softly.

James Kissane (8)
Pirton Hill Junior School

WHEN I WAS ALIVE

When I was one
I sucked my thumb
When I was two
I done up my shoe
When I was three
I banged my knee
When I was four
I touched the floor
When I was five
I learned to dive
When I was six
I picked up sticks

Victoria Green (11)
Pirton Hill Junior School

A Winter's Journey

Winter is Jack Frost's magic dust.
Winter is beautiful sunsets.
Winter is slippery roads.
Winter is gloves, coats, scarves and hats.
Winter is wooden sledges coming down hills.
Winter is large snowball fights.
Winter is thick frozen ponds.
Winter is bare fields.
Winter is ice skating.
Winter is a wonderland.
Winter is birds' footprints.
Winter is robin redbreast.
Winter is red balls of fire.
Winter is a silhouette against the sky.
Winter is freezing cold hands.
Winter is light ducks skating on frozen ponds.
Winter is packed snow.
Winter is snowflakes.
Winter is cold icicles.
Winter is the time I like best!

Fraser Cummings (8)
Polam Preparatory School

WINTER'S JOURNEY

Winter is wearing hats, gloves, coats and scarves.
Winter is Jack Frost's magic dust.
Winter is seeing the beautiful sunsets.
Winter is seeing ducks skating on ice.
Winter is thinking about wonderland.
Winter is playing in snow.
Winter is seeing bare trees.
Winter is birds' footprints everywhere.
Winter is icicles freezing solid.
Winter is snowdrops.
Winter is a ball of fire in the sky.
Winter is fluffy snow.
Winter is robins with red breasts.
Winter is slippery ice.
Winter is frozen ponds.
Winter is a cold time.
Winter is wrapping up warm.
Winter is sliding around.
Winter is going sledging.
Winter is my favourite time.

Hollie-Mae Hobbs (8)
Polam Preparatory School

WINTER'S JOURNEY

Winter is beautiful sunsets.
Winter is Jack Frost's magic dust.
Winter is redbreast robins.
Winter is skating on ponds.
Winter is winter wonderlands.
Winter is icicles hanging.
Winter is frozen ponds.
Winter is snow and ice.
Winter is frosty fields.
Winter is snowmen.
Winter is snow drifts.
Winter is snowdrops.
Winter is footprints in the snow.
Winter is slippery snow.
Winter is gloves, coats, scarves and hats.
Winter is skating on slippery ice.
Winter is fluffy sow falling.
Winter is twinkling woods.
Winter is woolly muffs.
Winter is freezing fields.
Winter is freezing cold weather!

Eleanor Polhill (8)
Polam Preparatory School

WINTER'S JOURNEY

Winter is snowdrops,
Winter is snowdrifts,
Winter is snowflakes,
Winter is Jack Frost's magic dust.
Winter is pond skating,
Winter is icicles,
Winter is beautiful sunsets,
Winter is a robin with a red breast,
Winter is slippery roads.
Winter is a wonderland.
Winter is silhouettes against the sky.
Winter is cold.
Winter is seeing the sun as a ball of fire.
Winter is warm gloves.
Winter is coats,
Winter is scarves,
Winter is hats,
Winter is sledges.
Winter is bare fields.
Winter is fluffy earmuffs.
Winter is ice.
Winter is hibernation.
Winter is a snowman.

Arjun Rai (8)
Polam Preparatory School

A WINTER'S JOURNEY

Winter is a wonderland
Winter is cold hands
Winter is snow drifts
Winter is packed snow
Winter is icicles
Winter is ice skating
Winter is fluffy snow
Winter is robin redbreast
Winter is frozen ponds
Winter is snowdrops
Winter is warm clothes
Winter is snowflakes
Winter is beautiful sunsets
Winter is Jack Frost's magic dust

Heather Stuckey (8)
Polam Preparatory School

WINTER'S JOURNEY

I like frost and snow
As well as beautiful sunsets.
Coats, gloves, scarves and hats
And days damp and wet.
Slippery
Sliding on the ice
A lot of packed snow.
A great ball of fire in the sky,
The opposite of down below.
Little robin redbreast
Bare fields and trees.
But then a fire and a mat
All just for me.

Ben Hollands (8)
Polam Preparatory School

A JOURNEY THROUGH WINTER

Gathering coats, gloves, scarves, skates and boots.
Out into the cold we go.
It's snowing!
The pond is frozen too.
'Skates out everybody!'
Snowdrops are falling,
Dawn is dawning,
Bed is awaiting us soon,
Morning will be here . . .

It's still snowing in the morning
Skating here we come!
Across the ice we go 'zoom zoom'
If we fall in, death will loom.

Sophie Willmott (8)
Polam Preparatory School

A JOURNEY THROUGH WINTER

Winter is slippery, sliding, ice
Winter is nice,
Ice skating!
Winter is bare, brown fields
Empty trees
Winter is Jack Frost's cold, magic dust
Winter is wonderful,
Red, green, orange, pink and yellow sunsets
Winter is a snowy wonderland
Whistling winds
Winter is frozen water
Winter is getting wrapped up warm.

Joshua Townson (8)
Polam Preparatory School

A WINTER'S JOURNEY

Snow drifts falling on your gloves
Watch out!
There's a snowball coming at you
Skating on frozen lakes,
Slippery, sliding, skidding around.
Robins flying
Showing off their big, red breasts.
Not many cars on the road.
I wonder why?
It's very slippery everywhere.
Children building snowmen in country fields.
Tapping trees so snow falls on your head.
It's getting late, let's go inside.
We can watch the sun set and rise.
Seeing robin's footprints on the ground.
Jack Frost had been last night.
Nothing can stop him now.

Jennifer Islip (9)
Polam Preparatory School

WINTER'S JOURNEY

Through winter's journey you will need gloves, coats, scarves and hats.
Winter is snow being gathered, packed and packed.
Winter hides the robin redbreast.
On the trees no leaves are left.
Winter is having warm clothes, hanging near the stove.
Winter has beautiful views, it seems like this world is new.
Winter is snowflakes dropping.
Winter is the sunshine stopping.
Winter makes frozen ponds.
For it to snow again I do long.

Alexander Monks (8)
Polam Preparatory School

WINTER'S JOURNEY

Winter is a wonderland.
Winter is cold, frosty and wet.
Winter is hats, coats, gloves and scarves.
Winter is white snow.
Winter is beautiful sunsets.
Winter is robins singing.
Winter is animals hibernating.
Winter is building snowmen.
Winter is snowballs.
Winter is Jack, Jack Frost.
Winter is ice.
Winter is ice hockey.
Winter is bare trees.
Winter is snowfalls.
Winter is frosty fields.
Winter is wonderful magical time.

Abigail Lavallin (8)
Polam Preparatory School

A JOURNEY THROUGH WINTER

In a journey through winter you would find soft snow.
In a journey through winter you would find snow drifts.
In a journey through winter you would find frozen ponds.
In a journey through winter you would find people skating happily.
In a journey through winter you would find lots of muffs.
In a journey through winter you would find icicles.
In a journey through winter you would find children on sledges.
In a journey through winter you would find snowmen on fluffy snow.
In a journey through winter you would find the sun looking like a ball
                    of fire.

Joseph Kearney (8)
Polam Preparatory School

WINTER'S JOURNEY

Winter is wonderland.
Winter is cold and frosty.
Winter is bare trees and fields.
Winter is icy roads.
Winter is snow drifts.
Winter is holly.
Winter is lovely sunsets.
Winter makes snowflakes fall down.
Winter is animals hibernating.
Winter is a snowland.
Winter is coats, gloves, scarves and hats.
Winter is a happy time.
Winter is building snowmen.
Winter is people having a good time on the ice.
Winter is Jack Frost's magic dust.
Winter is ice men.
Winter is icicles.
Winter is packs of snow.

Lewis Peat (8)
Polam Preparatory School

WINTER'S JOURNEY

Winter is a wonderful thing for
Winter has its ways
Its ways are cruel and frosty
But sometimes it can be nice
Because it does occasionally
Let a ray of sunshine
Hit the ground
And when it does, it gets a little warmer
But not a lot.

Edward Mahaffey (8)
Polam Preparatory School

WINTER'S JOURNEY

Cold, wild nights,
frosty icicles on my nose.
Ponds are frozen,
pipes are ice,
roads are slippery,
fluffy snow is white,
beautiful sunsets in the sky,
bare fields as white as can be,
snow drifts drifting from the sky,
animals are hibernating like my rabbit,
people have frozen hands,
Jack Frost's magic dust,
muffs on our frozen ears,
robin redbreast against the trees.
Wonderland is a cold, cold place
for people to go for a good, happy time,
gloves, coats, scarves and hats are very warm,
magic is all around us when winter's frost is here.
The sun looks like a ball of fire hanging in the sky!

Loran Wyatt (7)
Polam Preparatory School

THE SUNSHINE

The sun is shining brighter than a light,
the flowers glow as if never before,
the people wonder and children play and smile,
but ask yourself what will happen when it's gone,
the children wonder as they smile,
but still they wonder what or why.

Ruby Panesar (10)
Ramridge Junior School

A TYPICAL SCHOOL DAY

It's 7 o'clock
The alarm clocks ring
It's time to get up
I hear my mum sing

I go to the bathroom
And brush my teeth
Eat my breakfast
And knock for Keith

We walk to school
It's not too far
It's chilly this morning
I wish we had a car

We walk in the playground
And wait for the bell
The whistle is blown
It's Mr Patel

We all line up
And go into class
We all work hard
The days quickly pass

It's time to go home
It's half post three
We put on our coats
And go home for tea

I do my homework
And go out to play
Only in the garden
Not too far away

I hide in the shed
When mum shouts 'Bed!'

Dean Laird (10)
Ramridge Junior School

MY FEAR OF SPIDERS

My fear of spiders has not gone away,
It was all found out on one special day,
There I was, being a pain,
Too much attention I did gain,
The spider came from across the room,
There I was I felt doomed,
It came closer, I stepped back,
The bravery thing I did lack,
I jumped on the chair and heard a loud noise,
It came up and over all of the toys,
It looked at me and scuttled away,
I know it will come back some other day,
The noise is still there loud and clear,
Stop that screaming, Ticey, my dear!
The noise was my shrilling shrieking voice,
And believe me that voice was not my choice.

Ticey Ash (11)
Ramridge Junior School

ANIMALS

Cats and dogs,
Could be hogs,
Big frogs on little logs,
Up and down the garden,
Burp, the frog said, pardon.

Snails and slugs,
Eat some bugs,
All on a summer's day,
Some people could pay.

Cows and ants could be pants,
Ants are small and that means all,
And cows are humungously big.

Worms and bugs,
Worms give germs,
And bugs give hugs,
Worms are slimy,
And bugs are climby.

Pigs and monkeys,
Monkeys are slim,
And pigs are fat,
But they could turn into cats,
That's the end, goodbye.

Goodbye,
Hope to see you again,
We all had fun with the animals,
Goodnight
And good fight
See yah.

Rosie Mason (10)
Ramridge Junior School

ANIMALS IN THE FOREST

Animals in the forest,
Animals in the sea,
I have never seen them,
And they have never seen me.

Animals in the forest,
Animals in the woods,
Crocodiles, lizards and snakes live there,
I'm glad I don't live there, that's good.

Animals in the forest,
Animals in the trees,
Blackbirds make their nests out of twigs,
Surrounded by lots of bees.

Animals in the forest,
Animals in the holes,
All the animals hide away,
Like rabbits, hares and moles.

Animals in the forest,
Animals in the house,
Lots of different pets live there,
The cat always chases the mouse.

Animals in the forest,
Animals in the shed,
Many spiders live in here,
They use it for their bed.

Animals in the forest,
Animals round the bend,
I have come to the last line of my poem,
You could probably say it's the end!

Rebecca Long (9)
Ramridge Junior School

BULLYING

Bullying is such a horrible
Thing to do,
Although this may not really
Seem much to you.
This was a story that
Would never end,
Which kept on going on
And on around the bend.
Racism was one thing
I've got to mention,
Maybe they were just
Trying to get attention,
It hurt me so bad
As if someone had stabbed me,
I thought I was
Going mad, and that
No one would help me.
Then one day I realised
I could not cope anymore,
The pressure was so bad,
That I thought I would
Do something about it.
I thought to myself
How could I be such a clown?
And learn that you should stand up
For yourself.
And be proud for who you are.
Like I am myself.

Sarah Iqbal (10)
Ramridge Junior School

HOME

I am a pebble
Shiny red,
My home is on
The river bed.

I am a silver
Paper clip,
My home is on
A memo slip.

I am a yellow
Lollipop,
My home is in
A Village shop.

I am a towel
With strips of pink.
My home is by
The kitchen sink.

I am a golden
Twenty-four,
My home is on
An oaken door.

I am a kite
Of many hues,
My home is where
The wind should choose.

Amy Goodhew (9)
Ramridge Junior School

ALPHABET

A is for angel up in the sky.
B is for badger watching time fly.
C is for clown with a red nose.
D is for daffodils planted in rows.
E is for Ed the hedgehog so neat.
F is for flower so pretty and sweet.
G is for golf balls dropping into holes.
H is for hot dogs in freshly baked rolls.
I is for instrument to play at your leisure.
J is for jeep to ride in for pleasure.
K is for kite on a windy day.
L is for luggage when you go away.
M is for merry-go-round at the fair.
N is for nurse whose job is to care.
O is for office with papers to write.
P is for pillow fight during the night.
Q is for queuing when you move house.
R is for ruler to measure the mouse.
S is for Sam who waves from afar.
T is for Tom with his friend, the star.
U us for umbrella to keep off the rain.
V is for vicar with a baby again.
W is for wizard that makes dreams come true.
X, Y and Z are especially for you.

Reg Woollford (10)
Ramridge Junior School

FEELINGS FROM THE HEART

It's me, it's me,
with the sea,
sitting with glee
with the water rushing at my knees.
I did not care when people stared,
because I was happy inside,
and after all I still had my pride,
a soft tune played in my head,
I thought of happy things that had happened and been said,
and suddenly I sipped by tea,
with the water rushing at my knees.

Faye Rogan (10)
Ramridge Junior School

MY SISTER HOLLY

My sister Holly,
Is very jolly,
She always wears a wig,
When she does a jig,
When her dog barks,
She takes her down the park,
For a nice evening walk
And when she meets her friends,
She stops and talks and talks,
When Holly has gone for so long,
My mum says to me,
Go and fetch Holly for her tea.

Louise Davie (10)
St Margaret of Scotland RC Junior School

FUNNY OLD SHEEP

I have a lamb, a funny old lamb,
Who likes to eat turkey and ham!

I have a ewe, a funny old ewe,
Who only likes to wear one shoe!

I have a ram, a funny old ram,
Who likes to sleep in a pram!

I have three sheep, three funny old sheep,
Who only like to eat and sleep!

Ben Ryan (10)
St Margaret of Scotland RC Junior School

WHAT DOGS LIKE

Dogs are fun
they like to run
they like to bark
when they are
in the park.
They like to
chase cats
but they hate
smelly rats.
They like to
swim in lakes
but they hate
slimy snakes.

Naomi Cunningham (10)
St Margaret of Scotland RC Junior School

LOLLIPOP LADY

Lollipop lady, lollipop lady
When can I cross the road?
You can cross the road
When my stick goes bright green.
Lollipop lady
Lollipop lady
When can I tie my shoe laces?
You can cross the road
When my stick goes bright green.
Lollipop lady
Lollipop lady
Shush boy
Shush boy
Lollipop lady, when can I eat you?
Arrrrrr rrrrrh

Laura Catling (10)
St Margaret of Scotland RC Junior School

DREAMS

Gliding through the starry night,
All the rivers reflecting moonlight,
Softly feeling that gentle breeze,
Nothing stirs beneath the trees,
You see the stars softly shining,
And hear the wolf's howl and whining,
Suddenly you realise that it seems,
Yes, this is the place of your dreams.

Kayleigh Kerins (10)
St Margaret of Scotland RC Junior School

My Dad

My dad is always working,
And is hardly ever home
And even if he is,
He's always on the phone.

My dad is very funny,
He sings and tells us jokes,
The bad thing about my dad
Is that he drinks and smokes.

My dad's work is very far
That is why he has a company car,
I love it when my dad is here,
When he opens the door,
We all give a cheer.

When dad's angry he shouts 'Get up stairs',
We all rush up and say our prayers.

Stephanie Rankin (9)
St Margaret of Scotland RC Junior School

Baby Baby

Baby, baby, have some fun.
Baby, baby, don't lie in the sun.
Baby, baby, have a bun.
Baby, baby, don't suck your thumb,
Thumb, thumb.
Baby, baby, do that sum.
Baby, baby, don't play that drum.
Baby, baby, come over and sit with
Your old dear
          Mum.

Kelly Gethin (9)
St Margaret of Scotland RC Junior School

THE MAGIC CLOCK

I heard a clock
Go tickety tock
At twelve o'clock
There was a knock

I heard a clock
Go tickety tock
And to my shock
Elvis appeared in a frock!

I heard a clock
Go tickety tock
And there was a croc
Under my old sock

I heard a clock
Go tickety tock
At one o'clock

And guess what?

Out popped
A cuckoo!

Megan Moorhouse (9)
St Margaret of Scotland RC Junior School

FIREWORKS

Fireworks, fireworks, I like fireworks.
They spin and twirl high in the sky.
The Catherine wheel is really wicked.
It spins so fast you just can't miss it.
I like the bright colours, they're pretty and clear.
But when they go Bang! I cover my ears.

Amy O'Neill (10)
St Margaret of Scotland RC Junior School

A TIGER POEM

I watched it prowl upon its prey,
In a very special way,
Leap, pounce, with all its might,
Grips his prey very tight.

He drags his prey to his cave,
His family think he's very brave,
They savage up this ghastly meal,
Yum, yum, this is ideal!

The tiger is a ferocious beast,
And loves his daily feast,
It has bright orange fur,
Watch out in caves because that is where they lure.

I can tell you they're very scary,
But they're not too hairy,
Their black stripes stand out in the night,
But please keep out of his way, alright?

Its teeth are snow white
And so is its tummy.

I keep away from tigers in the night,
Because they might grip me very tight.
Roarrr!

Laura Murphy (11)
St Margaret of Scotland RC Junior School

FIZZY WIZZY

Fizzy, wizzy, fizzy wizzy,
lots of things are fizzy wizzy,
lemonade and orangeade and lots
more to choose from.

Fizzy wizzy, fizzy wizzy,
lots of things are fizzy wizzy,
cars, motorbikes, racing cars
and lots more to choose from.

Jodie Roberts (10)
St Margaret of Scotland RC Junior School

THE HOCKEY MATCH

Jogging around the pitch,
Feeling pain with a stitch,
The hockey teacher shrieks like a witch,
The warm-up goes without a hitch.

In a circle the team crowd,
No more chatting, we're not allowed,
The supporters shout out loud,
'Come on, Luton, make us proud.'

Hockey sticks made of wood,
Clean boots covered in mud,
Dodging as fast as we could,
Defending as we should.

Strips of red, green and black,
The crowd gathers at the back,
Shouting and screaming as we attack,
Hitting hard with our sticks we whack.

As we hear the final score,
Cheers of the crowd become a roar,
Up the league the team soar,
The best we are - you can't ignore!

Sophie Amos (10)
St Margaret of Scotland RC Junior School

THE TIGER

Something is moving through the tall, yellow grass,
Something bright ~
With claws of brass.

Coated the violent colour of fire and smoke,
Looking bright ~
With stripes of coke.

Two cruel eyes with a stone-cold look,
Dimly bright ~
Shaded like a rook.

A mouthful of razor-sharp, knife-like teeth,
Glimmering bright ~
Like the sun on the heath.

Something is moving through the tall, yellow grass,
Something bright ~
With claws of brass.

Paul Coy (10)
St Margaret of Scotland RC Junior School

WHAT ANIMAL?

Fearsome, terrible, nasty, have you got it?
Cunning, swift, strong, have you got it?
Sly, mean, cold-blooded, have you got it?
A predator of meat, have you got it?
Red and grey is his colour, have you got it?
It doesn't morph.
So it must be a *wolf!*

Sinéad Hegarty (10)
St Margaret of Scotland RC Junior School

THE STRANGER

The lady stood, a ghostly gleam in her eye,
Wild hair ran down to her thigh,
Her gown torn in places, on her foot a lump of mud,
On her cheek a splash of dry blood.

She moved in the phantom shadows of the old house,
Her wicked look could scare anyone from a giant to a mouse.
She dropped a dagger on the floor,
And looked around to the door.

Was she there for kill?
But was anybody there, in the old house on the hill?
But then, she ran, ran, ran out of the door,
She was last seen running across the moor.

Ruth Baker (10)
St Margaret of Scotland RC Junior School

THUNDER AND LIGHTNING

Thunder and lightning
Very, very frightening
People wake
Ground shook like an earthquake
People looking outside
Not even a bird could glide
There was a black sky
The weatherwomen told a lie
People shouting, how dare she
There are big black waves in the sea

Peter Gleasure (10)
St Margaret of Scotland RC Junior School

ALIENS ARE COMING

Aliens are everywhere, mostly in space,
They like to orbit the different planets like Mars,
And there's lots of mysterious tricks they like
For the aliens are coming.

There is a greasy-faced alien with spots on his chin,
He is big and strong with rusty foot skin,
He has the worst habits but he is quite skinny,
He likes to brush his teeth about once a year,
For the aliens are coming.

They are now on Mars, one planet to be,
They like to travel, as you can see,
They are close now from landing on Earth,
For they will place millions of mines,
On the innocent Earth,
For the aliens are closer.

The aliens are panicking,
They have no time left to do the mission,
For the aliens have gone,
And their mission has failed,
Everyone in Britain was happy to say the aliens have gone,
For the aliens have gone.

Liam Reddan (9)
St Margaret of Scotland RC Junior School

MY TEDDY

My teddy is lovely
I love him so much
I hug him and squeeze him
He's so soft to the touch

His name is Tedsy
And I take him everywhere
He's been in hospital with me
He kept me company there.

Daisy Monaghan (9)
St Margaret of Scotland RC Junior School

DISNEYLAND

I can't wait until I go on holiday to the USA
I will fly with Virgin all the way.
I will meet Mickey Mouse and have a chat
And hopefully he'll give me a souvenir hat
I'll go on the roller coasters and scream with delight
Then visit the haunted house and scream with fright.
My sister and I will go on all the rides
We better watch out when we go on the slides.
Maybe sometimes I'll sit by the pool
It certainly will help to keep me quite cool
I'm so excited I hardly can wait
But I'll have to, you see, it's going to be great!

James Sherry (10)
St Margaret of Scotland RC Junior School

MY DOG MONTY

My dog is big and hairy,
he's large and very scary,
only when he goes for walks,
never wants to stop for talks,
together we jump and play,
yet he knows home is not far away.

Mary-Ann Cheshire (9)
St Margaret of Scotland RC Junior School

BIRDS IN MY GARDEN

It's a cold, damp, yucky winter's day,
So I put bird feeders on the clothes line,
I watched quietly until the birds came,
The blue tits, green finches, hanging carefully, eating fine.

A pair of robins, a great tit and some bullfinches,
Come because they are starving hungry too,
Watch out, danger, fly away, panic, the cat's coming,
Up high to the sycamore trees they flew.

Squirrels and cats prowl, trying to get the birds,
Who keep warm by fluffing up their feathers,
Hope you like the yummy nuts and food I give you,
I'll try to feed you in all weathers.

Séamus Griffin (9)
St Margaret of Scotland RC Junior School

I THINK

I think I'd like to write a book
So everyone would come and look
And say well done! This book's great fun!
Why don't you write another one?
I'd write another one for them
So they might come and look again
And say, this girl deserves a prize
She should appear on 'Stars in their Eyes'.

Emily Donnellan (9)
St Margaret of Scotland RC Junior School

SCHOOL'S BORING, AS BORING CAN BE

School's boring, as boring can be,
Can't wait for them to set us free.
Friday's lunch just drags and drags,
The teacher always nags and nags,
About our decision to watch television
And not to do our long division.
He piles on homework sum after sum.
'Why are we so unlucky, how come?'
I start daydreaming about having wings,
Suddenly the school bell rings.
Thundering loudly we all cheer,
Don't care we've hurt the teacher's ear.
School's boring as boring can be,
But we don't care, for two days we're *free.*

Niamh Patton (9)
St Margaret of Scotland RC Junior School

MY TEDDY

Teddies, Teddies are so cute
My best Teddy is wearing a suit.
She is only five years old and
Once she had a cold.
I looked at her with my eyes
And I said, 'You poor little bear,
Your nose is runny,
I will get my mum to give you
Some lemon and honey.'

Joella Forsyth (9)
St Margaret of Scotland RC Junior School

THE TERRIBLE WEATHER

The rain gushing against the window,
The hailstones thumping on the ground.

The lightning flickering through the window,
The snow falling heavily on the ground.

The thunder shudders the window,
The lightning bouncing off the ground.

The sleet setting on the window,
The ice forming on the ground.

Snowed in past the windows,
The snow ten feet high on the ground.

Oh What Terrible Weather!

David Scott (9)
St Margaret of Scotland RC Junior School

PUDDLES

I love to splash in puddles
when the rain comes falling down
it's as good as lots of cuddles
or the laughter of a clown.

I jump into my yellow wellies
and run out the red door
my socks might end up smelly
or my toes might get sore.

Katie Sears (9)
St Margaret of Scotland RC Junior School

WHAT IS IT?

It is still and small
It can be short or tall
It's cuddly and bouncy
It's soft and furry

What is it?

It's got paws and ears
It's sometimes a he
Sometimes a she
It's good for playing
It's good for saying

What is it?

It's lovely
It's jubbly
It's cute and cuddly
and
It's my teddy bear!

Rebecca Byrne (10)
St Margaret of Scotland RC Junior School

MY FRIEND CODY

My friend's name is Cody
And she loves to pick her bogies.

She really is not nice
Because she likes to eat mice.

She has a big, long beard
So I guess she is just weird.

Kayleigh McLaughlin (10)
St Margaret of Scotland RC Junior School

WHY, MUM?

Wake up for your 9am feed,
Why, mum?
For that is a human need,
Why, mum?
That's the way we were made,
Why, mum?
Come along, we're being delayed,
Okay.

Get that food in your mouth, not on the wall!
Why, mum?
Oh stop it now, Paul!
Why, mum?
This can't go on!
Why, mum?
Come on. We should be gone!
Sorry, mum.

We'll go for a stroll in the park
Why, mum?
Hurry up, before it gets dark,
Why, mum?
Now wrap up warm,
Why, mum?
They forecast a storm!
Really?

Mum, we must get under a tree!
Why, son?

Alessandra Doogan (9)
St Margaret of Scotland RC Junior School

THE TIGER

Tiger, tiger in the moonlight
Tiger, tiger standing straight and tall
Tiger, tiger colourful and bright
Tiger, tiger big and small.

Slowly striding in the night
With its big black claws
Ready to pounce on his prey
Like an eagle in the sky.

Its teeth are the size of a dagger
They're white and shine in the night
They're sharp and prickly like a shark
They could tear the flesh of polar bears.

His body is like a beam of light
It's quick, it's fast, it's full of energy
I wonder if anyone would go
Quite so near to this so beautiful, so dangerous creature.

Now he has met his future wife
They should be together all their life
Many young ones that they will have soon
To hunt and scavenge by the light of the moon.

Tiger, tiger in the moonlight
Tiger, tiger standing straight and tall
Tiger, tiger colourful and bright
Tiger, tiger big and small.

Maria Cortese (10)
St Margaret of Scotland RC Junior School

WHEN I AM OLD

When I am old I am going to have some fun
I will wear shorts and a vest in the winter
And in the summer I will wear a fleece and a pair of trousers
And stand in wet cement.
I will eat lots of fatty food
And run around in my shorts when it is raining
I will learn to spit
And drive a motorbike
And eat chocolate for every meal of the day.

When I am old I will go to Brazil
And climb trees and eat coconuts until my heart is content
I will ride down the road on my bike and pull wheelies
And ride roller-skates.

When I am old I will go to the park
Play on the swings and whiz down the slide
I will steal metal dustcaps off cars
And make snow angels in the snow
I will go swimming and do somersaults into the water
And dive off the diving board
This is what I will be like when I am old
So watch out, *here I come!*

Luke Sears (10)
St Margaret of Scotland RC Junior School

TIME

Places to see
People to meet
There is so little time
And what I want
Most of all is for
Time not to pass me by

People rushing here
People rushing there
People rushing everywhere
I just stand and stare
Time is so precious.

Daniel Panepinto (10)
St Margaret of Scotland RC Junior School

THE TREE BOA

The Tree Boa waits for a bird to fly,
The bird takes no notice of the monkey's cry.
The bird goes off to make a nest,
The snake appears to have a rest.
The bird keeps going on making a nest,
The snake carries on appearing to rest.
The bird steps back to admire his work,
But he doesn't know who will lurk.
The bird flies through a hollow log,
But sees nothing except a frog.
The bird sees an insect in a groove,
The snake now knows where the bird will move.
But the snake is wrong, the bird won't move,
Towards the insect in the groove.
The bird flies back up to the nest,
The snake appears to have a rest.
Then it hits the snake in the head,
Could he eat something else instead?
The snake thinks of a roaring blizzard.
He's off to go and eat a lizard.

Ziedo Solomon (10)
St Margaret of Scotland RC Junior School

WHAT YOU DO DURING SCHOOL

Come along, children,
The bell has rung,
Line up nicely,
Do try to get along.

We're in the classroom,
Please sit down,
I'll take the register,
Oh, children, do not frown.

English has started,
T S Eliot we'll read,
Poems he wrote and facts we'll read,
Oh, children, we should take the lead.

The bell has rung for break,
You can't go out,
It's raining you see,
So stay and tour about.

The end of break has come,
Get in your seat,
I'll send the monitors up,
You better do as I say Pete.

The teacher comes back,
With maths she seeks,
Number lines she has found,
All in the class are weak.

The bell has rung for lunch,
Go straight in,
You shouldn't hang around,
You should win.

Claire Legg (10)
St Margaret of Scotland RC Junior School

THE TIGER

Tiger, tiger in the night
Catching seagulls in a bite
Catch one whole, catch one small
Tiger is happy, curls in a ball

What would it do if it meets a bear?
Most probably run as fast as a hare
Run to a cave and get a scare
See a bat with humungous hair

Goes back home, there's no bear
Goes to bed, sees a hare
Has a nightmare about a bear
Wakes up with a scare

Stripes orange, black and red
Sees a monster under the bed
Runs out and dives into a hedge
He looks in and can't find a thing

Goes back to bed, finds a sledge
Goes down a mountain like a fountain
He counts the rocks while he is falling
He looks like he is scolding

Tiger, tiger in the night
Catching seagulls in a bite
Catch one whole, catch one small
Tiger is happy, curls in a ball

James McGuinness (10)
St Margaret of Scotland RC Junior School

MY BEST FRIEND

We'd been best friends since we were four,
But we wouldn't see each other any more.
We'd played together in the sun,
We laughed, we squealed, we had some fun.

We had a leaving party in our class,
We sat and ate on the fresh-cut grass.
I tried to be happy and forced a smile,
But I knew you were leaving in a little while.

I'd helped you get your suitcase packed,
Ready to load on an aeroplane rack.
You gave me Bubbles, your old teddy bear,
I gave you a necklace, just to be fair.

The 'for sale' sign's not there any more,
There's a different family behind your door.
Now your house is an empty place,
Whenever I see it, I miss your face.

I sleep with Bubbles every night,
I close my eyes and squeeze him tight.
As long as I hold him, it isn't the end,
You'll always be the world's best friend.

It makes my day to hear the postman call,
When I see the envelope laid in the hall.
You always have so much to say,
And I know we'll meet again some day.

Leana Brady (9)
St Margaret of Scotland RC Junior School

CAN I HAVE . . .

'*Mum*
Can I have a
brown and white puppy
and a goldfish?
If you don't let me I'll ask
        Dad instead.'
        '*No!*'

    '*Dad*
    Can I have a brown and white puppy
    And two goldfish?
    If you don't let me I'll ask
      Nan instead.'
        '*No!*' (I know she'll let me)

'*Nan*
Can I have a brown and white puppy
And three goldfish?
If you don't let me, can I have
        100
            quid?'
        'Yes, here you go.'

So I bought a little puppy and four lovely fish.
No I don't need to ask for
        Another
            100 quid.

Trixie Thomas (10)
St Margaret of Scotland RC Junior School

THE TIGER

Hunting human with a knife
running tiger for its life.
In the forest is where it rests
ready to pounce at its best.

He who looks in the tiger's eye
will be the one who will bleed and die.
Ripping, biting at his skins
the tiger is the one who wins.

The tiger's eyes are blazing hot
bubbling up in a boiling pot.
Tigers always get so mad
that they bite to pieces very bad.

The tiger lives on blood and meat
and eats its prey nice and neat.
It survives in its cosy lair
but going to sleep is very rare.

All night long it hunts for food
but never gets in a mood.
Wild and vicious, a fierce creature
but really it has a scary feature.

Hunting human with a knife
running tiger for its life.
In the forest is where it rests
ready to pounce at its best.

Alex Bruckshaw (11)
St Margaret of Scotland RC Junior School

THE TIGER

Tiger, tiger in the night
shining like fire ever so bright
with a sparkle in his eyes
he will pounce like a killer

Human eyes gaze upon
a little killer is born
so cute and furry, what a surprise
but a little killer in his eyes

A tiger looks very delightful
but it really is very frightful
a tiger is very suspicious
also it is very vicious

Hands made this creature
but while it waits it has no feature
a tiger may look very mild
but it is very wild

Tigers always scratch and fight
they often do it with a lot of might
a tiger catches his food fast
he never gets there last

Tiger, tiger in the night
shining like fire ever so bright
with a sparkle in his eyes
he will pounce like a killer

Ryan McLean (10)
St Margaret of Scotland RC Junior School

THE TIGER

Tiger, tiger burning bright
Lurking in the night
He is very angry indeed
So don't try anything silly

The tiger insisted that you stay
If you don't he'll make you pay
As it takes a tremendous leap
Around the grass he shall creep

'My fangs are very scary,
My fur is very hairy,
You better watch out, here I come
Or I'll bite you, eat you and put you in my tum.'

If it gets in a hard fight
It will end as the brave knight
If it gets in a bad mood
It shall look for some food

If you're hiding in a jeep
You're the thing it's going to keep
You should live in fear
If you're very near

Tiger, tiger burning bright
Lurking in the night
He is very angry indeed
So don't try anything silly

Curtis Headley (11)
St Margaret of Scotland RC Junior School

THE TIGER

Tiger, tiger in a fight
What does happen in the moonlight?
Rabbits run through the trees
As the tiger roars like a cannon

Burning, oranges, yellows and reds
Piercing, screaming eyes of threads
Ravishing, violent shiny eyes
Closed as the sleeping fire lies

Stripes of dark, dark black
Oranges and reds cover its back
It's white shiny teeth gleaming
While the prey is screaming.

Scream, it bites the head
Scream, the prey is dead
Ripping flesh everywhere
The fire has killed the bear

Its eyes are gleaming
Its breath is foaming
As it jumps and bounces
Then it crouches and pounces

Tiger, tiger in a fight
What does happen in the moonlight?
Rabbits run through the trees
As the tiger roars like a cannon

Danny Prendergast (11)
St Margaret of Scotland RC Junior School

THE TIGER

Tiger, tiger in a fight
Tiger, tiger fights till night
He bites and jumps
He pounces and thumps. Not surprised he's in a grump.

He waits for prey
And he waits all day
Then along runs a hare
With a frightful scare. Would you like to be there?

The jungle's awakened by his roar
Time for lunch, he has a boar
His eyes are gleaming
His breath is steaming.

All is silent
But still is violent
He looks nice
But he'll tear you in one slice.

Behind a tree it lies in shadows
Resting his aching sinews
He's stopped the striding
And the colliding.

Tiger, tiger in a fight
Tiger, tiger fights till night
He bites and jumps
He pounces and thumps. Not supervised he's in a grump.

Michael McPoland (10)
St Margaret of Scotland RC Junior School

THE TIGER

Tigers, tigers so big and brave
Have you wondered how they behaved?
They only feed on human flesh
They're very cautious animals.

Their eyes are a beamy red
Their black stripes go over its head
Their orange fur is so bright
They climb up trees by adapting its height.

While hunting their eyes shrink
They run as fast as I could blink
They tear through the gruesome flesh
Leaving only a little mess.

Their fierce eyes look at your neck
Then they take a little peck
They lick their lips after the meal
Then lie on grass curled up like a wheel.

They are not as fierce as you may think
They are important in the food link
Their coat is camouflaged
But they don't need it, they're too large!

Tigers, tigers so big and brave
Have you wondered how they behaved?
They only feed on human flesh
They're very cautious animals.

Sinead Kelly (11)
St Margaret of Scotland RC Junior School

THE TIGER

Tigers, tigers beaming eyes,
In the long grass he lies,
Its springy hind legs spring to its prey,
As it hunts through the night.

Its fur is soft and lovely to hold,
Tigers' stripes as black as mould,
He's quick on his feet,
He will never be beat.

His feet paw prints are a sign,
Of danger usually in a line,
It means he is lurking,
Near or far, nobody's looking.

It pounces on its prey,
Nearly every single day,
His eyes are brilliant far to see,
They glow yellow, orange, fiery.

It's cute when it's a baby,
But he could stay maybe,
I hope he won't be a killer,
Because I'll hide behind a pillar.

Tigers, tigers beaming eyes,
In the long grass he lies,
Its springy hind legs spring to its prey,
As it hunts through the night.

Siobhan Bradley (11)
St Margaret of Scotland RC Junior School

THE TIGER

His colour is so bright,
Like a blooming red light,
Flaming red, orange, gold,
And bright as can be.

His eyes are big and bright,
So that they can see at night,
Look left and then right,
And then run with a fright.

He lives in the forest,
With animals so fierce,
That hide at night,
With their ears pierced.

His paws are so big,
With claws so sharp,
That they will cut
You right in half.

He goes slow to his prey,
That they don't have a lot to say,
He runs so quick,
That they can't see him kick.

His colour is so bright,
Like a blooming red light,
Flaming red, orange, gold,
And bright as can be.

Laura Kelly (10)
St Margaret of Scotland RC Junior School

TIGERS

Tigers, tigers in the night
do they give you a fright?
Slowly it takes long strides
then it can see you with its eyes.

In the morning its eyes are red
I wouldn't like its teeth near my head.
His eyes are beaming
and his breath is steaming.

His teeth are sharp
when they stab through your heart.
He runs like a shock of light
but when he comes near he starts to bite.

In the hot blazing sun he sleeps
and in the night he creeps.
Through the jungle it stalks
across the stream he walks.

Tigers, tigers in the night
do they give you a fright?
Slowly it takes long strides
then it can see you with its eyes.

Danny Llambias (10)
St Margaret of Scotland RC Junior School

FRACTIONS

In maths today we did fractions,
nobody liked them at all,
you could tell by all their actions,
they definitely didn't like fractions.

Thankfully we had a fire drill,
that was a definite thrill,
until we got back,
we had an extra hour of fractions.

Caitlin Flanagan (10)
St Margaret of Scotland RC Junior School

FIVE DAYS IN SCHOOL

I woke up on Monday, I felt quite happy
        But then I knew I had to go to school
I walked through the hall, got hit by a ball
        So that was Monday at school.

On Tuesday I got told off by the head
        I didn't do my homework
When I got home I went straight to bed
        And that was Tuesday at school.

Wednesday, swimming
        I started singing
I was having fun
        But then I got done
On Wednesday at school.

On Thursday, PE
        What luck for me.
That's Thursday at school.

The week is nearly done
        Friday has come.
Home time is here.
        That's my week at school.

Courtney Lee (10)
St Margaret of Scotland RC Junior School

TIGER

Orange and black I see
Beautiful and proud is he
Roaring through the dark, thick jungle
With his glowing, ginger eyes

Up in the mountains he stays
As still as a mouse he lays
For the jungle is below
For he is the king of all

Slowly creeping through the wood
Trying to catch his food
What shall he find?
Maybe a big surprise

His claws are fierce and sharp
As a song drifts like a harp
His teeth are yellow and dark
As the night thickness the darkness

I love the way his heart beats
His fur is so soft and neat
His roar is loud and fearful
It makes me go all tearful

Orange and black I see
Beautiful and proud is he
Roaming through the dark, thick jungle
With his glowing, ginger eyes.

Victoria Mizsei (10)
St Margaret of Scotland RC Junior School

THE TIGER

The tiger's eyes are beautiful and bright,
but not as fierce as his bite.
He may look like a lost bumble bee,
but on the inside he is fierce and deadly.

His eyes glow like a burning fire,
but to have his fur is my desire.
His body is sleek with stripes so grand,
to be his friend I do command.

He sneaks about,
and pounces fast.
To hunt his prey,
he will get at last.

In the jungles of Africa and Asia too,
in Kenya's safari and London zoo.
In all these places the tiger is found,
the king of the jungle, his favourite surround.

He is as gentle as a pussy cat,
and his fur is as soft as a mat.
The tiger runs free,
over land we can see.

The tiger's eyes re beautiful and bright,
but not as fierce as his bite.
He may look like a lost bumble bee,
but on the inside he is fierce and deadly.

Cathriona Lane (10)
St Margaret of Scotland RC Junior School

THE TIGER

The tiger steps on the ground so dry.
It's so hot that we could die.
He runs around and goes to kill
To make his tummy fill.

He has bright eyes
That glow in the moonlit skies.
They are like burning fire
If you say You're not scared, you're a liar.

He has beautiful fur
That might not occur
To killers. His fur is soft and cuddly
But don't touch him, he's not very friendly.

His intentions to kill are very high.
Some people have had a try
But did they come back? No.
His intentions to kill are high not low.

So you see this tiger is not kind.
Take this to mind.
If you see a tiger who's not been fed
Run away before you're . . . dead.

The tiger steps on the ground so dry.
It's so hot that we could die.
He runs around and goes to kill
To make his tummy fill.

Rebecca Dillon (11)
St Margaret of Scotland RC Junior School

THE TIGER

Searching through the jungle on a cold, wet night
Going through the trees on the left, on the right
Stepping through bushes as quiet as a mouse
Then I find what I'm looking for, finally a tiger.

Under the tree it looks so huge and bright
And just lying there as quiet as the night
At any time it could jump out and roar
And swipe me across the chest with his big colossal claw.

The tiger then suddenly gave me a look
But I just stood there and immediately shook
The tiger stood up and showed me his jaws
And it stood up on its big, black claws.

Maybe it will come up to me and walk straight past
But then he might chase through the jungle very fast
It stares at me with one unwinking eye
Maybe I'll run away, I'm sure I might try.

Will the tiger run quickly away
But then he might possibly stay
I'm sure I'm in a frightful mood
But then it walks away to find some food.

Searching through the jungle on a cold, wet night
Going through trees on the left, on the right
Stepping through bushes as quiet as a mouse
Then I find what I'm looking for, finally a tiger.

Luke Brawley (11)
St Margaret of Scotland RC Junior School

MY CAT SMOKEY

My cat Smokey
he does the okey kokey
I think he has a girlfriend
unless they call them furfriends

He was a cat, she was a cat
both as black as a witch's hat
and down in the basket they did dwell
and loved each other very well

They loved each other very well
Very well, very well
and nobody loves my cat
As much as me
As much as me.

Chelsey McLoughlin (10)
St Margaret of Scotland RC Junior School

ALL ABOUT EASTER

Easter eggs you eat,
cards nice and neat,
newborn animals like chicks,
inside an egg it kicks,
little Easter treats,
families meet,
wrappers of eggs and little children,
shiny and beautiful is Easter day,
I wish Easter could stay.

Louise Currant (9)
St Margaret of Scotland RC Junior School

POETIC VOYAGE

I'm packing my suitcase as quick as I can
I can't wait to get there and catch a sun-tan
I'm ready now, I just can't wait,
We're getting in the car now, it's going to be great.

Just three hours left then we'll be there
I wonder if there's jellyfish, I don't really care;
My brother thinks he's going to meet a bar,
But all I want to listen to is the sea when we get there.

Just half an hour left, I can't take it anymore
All that's in my head is *'the seashore'*
My baby sister's playing with her toys,
And my mum is singing, making *lots* of noise.

I went to sleep and when I woke up
All I could hear was the seagulls above.

Tia Doris (10)
Sundon Park Junior School

MY GRAN

My gran is as fat as an elephant!
Her hair is like a fox curled up on her head.
Her eyes are like black circles on a stick.
Her face is like a cracked mountain.
When she walks she is like a kangaroo.
When she sits she is like a soldier.
When she laughs she is like a witch.
When she sleeps she is like Snorlax.
The best thing about my gran is:
She's the best gran in the world!

Rebecca Quille (8)
Sundon Park Junior School

THE WIND

I meanly blow at the large oak trees
And watch them drop their leaves.

As I creep into cracks and windows
Folk cover my entrance cold-heartedly.

I help kites blow into the blue
Cloudy sky.

I tug fiercely at the curtains and
Knock over precious ornaments.

Once have calmed down
I sleep quietly in the sky.

Yasmin Adnan (10)
Sundon Park Junior School

THE WIND

I can whistle through black forests,
without waking any sleeping birds.

I can shake tall buildings,
giving them no mercy.

I can rip down any tree,
shredding any branch.

I can howl savagely through magnificent towns,
ripping off rooftops.

When I have finished my devastating destruction,
I disappear off to the serene misty mountain.

David Murray (11)
Sundon Park Junior School

MY GRAN

My gran is as nice as my dad.
Her hair is combed down as a
field which has been cut by a
tractor.
Her eyes are like a shiny
brown gemstone.
Her face is as smooth as a door.
When she walks she is as smart
as a butler.
When she sits she looks as
Comfortable as her dog
Charlie.
When she laughs she looks
as happy as me.
When she sleeps she is like a
Whistle of a referee.
The best thing about my gran
Is when she gives me sweets.

Kurtis Huckle (8)
Sundon Park Junior School

THE WIND

I can sneakily and silently slip through windows.
I can lift oak trees with my powerful gust.
I can knock down old ladies.
I can knock fences over without anyone knowing.
I can topple boats in the sea.
I can blow through forests without birds waking.

Jamie Recardo (10)
Sundon Park Junior School

THE WIND

I can scatter all the crinkly leaves,
And pull the tree-trunks off.

Make blizzards as cold as snow
And hurricanes as loud as exploding volcanoes.

I can run as fast as zooming rockets
But walk as slow as a sly fox.

When I am happy I dance around like a queen,
But when I am sad I destroy cities.

Now the day is coming to an end
And I can zoom straight off to sleep.

Zena Adams (10)
Sundon Park Junior School

FIREWORKS

Fireworks are loud, bright and colourful,
Fireworks are big, exciting and full of fun.

Sparklers sparkling bright in the night,
People getting burnt for they have no gloves.

Rockets soaring up in the night sky,
A loud bang and an explosion of colour.

Bangers, banging and fountains spraying colour high,
Colours falling from the sky.

That's what fireworks night is all about.

Christopher Clarke (11)
Sundon Park Junior School

MY GRAN

My gran is almost as old as the Queen.
Her hair is like an elephants wrinkly trunk.
Her eyes are like round meatballs.
Her face is like furry tiger's back.
When she walks she is like a monkey
Looking for its food.
When she sits she is like a bent toothpick.
When she laughs she is like a hyena coughing.
When she sleeps she is like a train hooting
And an owl at the same time.
The best thing about my gran is that
She gives me presents.

Holly Elliott (9)
Sundon Park Junior School

POETIC VOYAGES

Across the gentle waves of the sea,
Alone on the ship, just you and me,
The sky is starting to get dark,
Fireworks are starting to spark,
Pink and yellow, green and blue,
Wow! That's fantastic, even in the dew,
It seems to be getting thicker, lovely white fog,
The Loch Ness monster on that log,
Now we're coming into the bay,
Of the waters of Loch Tay,
I know I may never see you again,
So we'll say goodbye,
My dear friend.

Susanna Butler (10)
Sundon Park Junior School

The Terrifying Rain

I shoot down like an arrow,
I hit the ground like a knockout
I can flood the towns
I drown people
I can drench clothes
I can shoot raindrops from the sky
I can race through a keyhole
I will dribble down raincoats
I will make puddles to splash in
Then I stop slowly
I am called the rain

Jonathon Butler (10)
Sundon Park Junior School

Fireworks

F   ireworks zooming up to Mars,
I   n the bright night sky.
R   ed, yellow, green and blue,
E   ndless fun!
W   onderful colours!
O   range, purple, brown and gold,
R   ainbow colours in the moonlit sky, as,
K   etchup-coloured sparkles,
S   parkle in the sky.

Aamenah Hawash (10)
Sundon Park Junior School

HOME TIME

It's another day at school,
And I'm acting like a fool.
I can't do my work,
And boy, am I a jerk!
I've been told off already,
But I'm trying to keep it steady.
To think school has just started,
And I wish I could be parted.
It's just half past nine,
And I can't wait for home time!

Carla Pointing (11)
Sundon Park Junior School

POETIC VOYAGE

I'm flying on an aeroplane
far across the sea;
The clouds are white and fluffy
looking up at me.

I watch the seas go by me
I'm flying through the air,
I wonder what it will be like
when I finally get there?

Kirstie Galvin (10)
Sundon Park Junior School

MY GRAN

My gran is as old as the queen.
Her hair is like worms dancing on the top of her head.
Her eyes are like little white footballs.
Her face is like a wrinkly elephant.
When she walks she is like a slow slug.
When she sits she is like she's sinking in quicksand.
When she laughs she is like a cackling old witch.
When she sleeps she is like an elephant blowing his trunk.
The best thing about my gran is
Whenever she comes round she always buys me something.

Peter Bywaters (8)
Sundon Park Junior School

MY GRAN

My gran is as old as a scraggy old cat.
Her hair is like old wiggly worms.
Her eyes are like cold ice.
Her face is like an old wrinkly bag.
When she walks she is like a caterpillar.
When she sits she is like a question mark.
When she laughs she is like a witch.
When she sleeps she is like a pig.
The best thing about my gran is that she gives me money.

Katie Hughes (8)
Sundon Park Junior School

MY GRAN

My gran is as old as the whole universe.
Her hair is like a curly cauliflower.
Her eyes are like a vampire's eyes when they need to suck blood.
Her face is like fire burning.
When she walks she is like the men in black.
When she sits it's like she has got ants in her pants.
When she laughs she is like a pig snoring.
When she sleeps she is like a horse snorting.
The best thing about my gran is everything.

Luke Horan (8)
Sundon Park Junior School

MY GRAN

My gran is as old as an ancient pyramid.
Her hair is like an old dirty rag bag.
Her face is like a screwed up piece of paper.
When she walks she is like an old slow worm.
When she sits she is like an old slow Jack in a box going down.
When she laughs she is like an evil witch who is plotting a plan.
When she is asleep she is like a woodpecker that is trying to make a
              nest.
The best thing about my gran is that she tells me lots of tricks.

Michael Sibley (8)
Sundon Park Junior School

MY GRAN

My gran is as small as a jockey.
Her hair is like new-made thread.
Her eyes are like little sweet balls.
Her face is like crinkly crisps from a shop.
When she walks she is like a new-born turtle.
When she sits she is like a dustpan under a stair.
When she laughs she is like a playing band.
When she sleeps she is like a noisy tiger.
The best thing about my gran is that
She gives me money, and foods I like!

Lee Wilkinson (8)
Sundon Park Junior School

THE WIND

I can march around like a one man army,
I roar and growl like a fearsome beast.
I can push and pull up huge great trees.
I can whip up spray from seas and oceans,
I can send ships down to the depths.
I can rave and riot and turn over cars,
I can strip trees of all their leaves.
I kick up dust clouds like a mischievous child,
And I slam doors like a raging adult.
But when I am calm I can stay quiet as a mouse.

Matthew Liam Gander (11)
Sundon Park Junior School

MY MUM

My mum loves me.
She is a busy bee.
She does the cooking.
She makes the pudding.
Then she makes a cup of tea.
She goes in a car.
She goes really far.
She goes in and out.
She goes all about.
I love my mum.
She does it all for free.

Craig Komlos (10)
Weatherfield School

THE NEW BABY

Baby, baby, what will it be?
It is growing in a tummy.
I am so excited I just can't wait.
Will it be a boy?
Will it be a girl?
I wonder what it will be.
I am going to play with the baby.
I am going to give the baby hugs.
I reckon it will be the most beautiful baby in the world.

Lee Huggins (11)
Weatherfield School

MICHAEL OWEN

I like Michael Owen
He has good football skills.
He does brilliant penalties
He is a football star.
He plays for Liverpool
And England too.
I would like to be Michael Owen.

Shaun Ayles (10)
Weatherfield School

MY BROTHER

My brother gave me sweets.
My brother played with me.
My brother gave me treats.
My brother gave me money
and he hugged me.
We went on our bikes.
I miss him.

Daniel Banks (11)
Weatherfield School

MY LITTLE BROTHER

My little brother, he's so mad.
Mum can't even change his nappies.
He's so mad it will take an army
To change his nappy.
Wait! Not even an army can change his nappy.
But somehow mum does it.
I don't know.

Gareth Glanville (10)
Weatherfield School

MY COUSIN

My cousin is cool.
He always rides his skateboard
round my house.
He plays hockey.
But he beats up my dad.
His name is Conor.
He is amazing.

Michael Murphy (10)
Weatherfield School

MY NAN

My nan buys me sweets.
I sleep at her house.
My nan cooks me dinner.
She plays games with me.
I love my nan so much. She loves me.
She buys me some magazines.
I love my nan.

Samantha Rich (11)
Weatherfield School

MY FAVOURITE FOOTBALLER

My favourite footballer
Is David Beckham.
Oh, David, how could you
Lose the football match?
You only scored four,
You usually score more.

Jayce Minnis (10)
Weatherfield School

MY LITTLE COUSIN

My little cousin Megan
She's a little star
She smiles at me when I pick her up
But dribbles and says ha ha!
My little cousin Megan
She won't ever tell
She's sometimes good, she's sometimes bad
But she rings a bell!

James Swain (10)
Weatherfield School

MY BROTHER

My brother is called Mark.
He is seven.
He's bossy and messes up my room.
Mum and me say, 'go away,
we are doing the tea
and you can't draw in my colouring book.'
He is a nuisance.

Laura Taylor (11)
Weatherfield School

MY BROTHER

My brother makes me cross.
He comes into my room.
My brother is annoying.
He takes my CD player.
I say go away.
But he is sometimes nice to me.

Hayley Rogers (11)
Weatherfield School

MY MUM

Is she good?
        Yes
Does she care?
        Yes
Is she the best?
        Yes
Does she give me food?
        Yes
Is she a good mum?
        Yes!

Jake Watts (11)
Weatherfield School

ONCE IN A LIFETIME VOYAGE

Don't just sit down
Don't have a doubt
It's really great
Much better than work or school
And you might get in the record books
That's not just for your good looks.

V   isiting places you've never been
O   verjoyed with what you see
Y   ellow, red, blue, it's a wonder
A   nd no time to sit and ponder
G   ulping down packets of food
E   nough to get you out of a mood
S   pace voyages.

Bethany Robins (10)
William Austin Junior School

THE VOYAGE OF A LIFETIME

'Twas the day of the spaceship inspection
When the pilot had an ear infection
And the crew needed a replacement
The only person they found lived in a basement
The inspector needed a ride
So they flew away over the tide

They flew over to Mars
With their rations of chocolate bars
When someone started shooting the spaceship
They had to quickly do a giant flip
The pilot got an 'A'
Because he got them away

Zeshan Rasul (10)
William Austin Junior School

MY SPACE WISH

One night I looked up in the sky,
Then I wished that I could fly.
I would go up there in a big spaceship,
Boy, then my grandma's wig will flip!
I could go up there and walk on the moon,
And act just like a silly goon.
I'd go up there and sit on Mars,
And then look up at all the stars.
For hours I'll float around the sun,
Oh boy, oh boy would that be fun!
To be up there alone in space,
And look at the Earth's lovely face.
To be in space for ages to sail,
But forever more, my wish will fail.

Lorraine Ford (9)
William Austin Junior School

POETIC VOYAGES

'Did you see that?'
'Did you see that?' people ask.
While I wonder, in space people ponder
While facing upwards to Mars,
I look at the stars,
Trying to spot that incredible ship,
Flying across the sky past Saturn.

While I can see the pattern of the
Crusader fighting the monster.
When the monster was defeated by the
Crusader's efforts.

The people of Neptune were able to fetch
Their long lost victory and sold it for gold.
Hurray!

Sehrush Hussain (10)
William Austin Junior School

POETIC VOYAGES

V   oyages are fun when in space,
O   h you have a pink face.
Y   ou, you are an . . . *alien!*
A   nd your name is . . . Damion.
G   osh! So what's life like?
E   xtremely boring, I think I'm on a hike.
S   uddenly I think it's a race
    . . . and I can't keep up the pace!

Gareth Ireson (9)
William Austin Junior School

ᴄLUMBUS AND CAPTAIN COOK

ꓸden ships,

meat,
been there,

ꓸmes along Captain Cook,
ꓸs and limes,
ꓸe poor scurvy-ridden sailors,
ꓸg at sea.

ꓸopher Columbus and Captain Cook,
ꓸrs through a lifetime,
ꓸile at risk on high seas,
ꓸid not suffer the same scene!

Frances Ryan (10)
William Austin Junior School

MY VOYAGE

M y ship voyage turned to a disaster
Y elled everyone as the ship got faster
V ictory we had not from the storm
O ver the seas it became dawn
Y elped and cried everyone for help
A nswers we had not to be helped
G lued we were to the chilly ship
E ventually the ship began to rip
  Then we passed off with a
  traditional burial at sea.

Jawad Safdar (10)
William Austin Junior School

POETIC VOYAGES

T ourist, travellers are travelling.
R oads, which way? Left or right?
A ll are buckled up in their seatbelts and ready to go.
V oyages sometimes get boring so play a game.
E ndless journeys go on and on but you finally get there.
L ong roads seem like they never end.
L ong journeys seem like they never end.
I nside the car it gets so hot and sweaty.
N ever fall asleep while driving.
G oing places doesn't have to be in a car.

Alex Morrissey (9)
William Austin Junior School

SPACE

S is for the brilliant stars that shine through your heart
P is for the planets that are so far away
A is for the aliens that have very funny eyes
C is for the space craft that flies so far away
E is for the Earth which is the best place to be in the whole of space!

Danielle James (10)
William Austin Junior School

PLANETS

Planets are in space
The Earth's a planet, it's great
Planets are so great

Jaleesa Evelyn (10)
William Austin Junior School

SPACE TRAVEL

I'm going to Space,
For a big race.
I'm going to the Space Station,
To put on my bike a playstation.
The race is tomorrow,
I haven't any gas, I shall borrow.
Oh no, the race is today,
What shall I do and what shall I say?
I saw a big alien sitting next to me,
I come in peace, I said, as you can see.
1, 2, 3, *bang,* go,
Everyone zoomed off, I went so slow.
Everyone else's gas ran out, they slowed down,
I ran passed them and gave them a frown.
I was beginning to run out of gas soon,
I remembered I borrowed some and put it in before noon.
I zoomed off like a rocket,
Until someone pulled the plug out of the socket.
My dad ran and put it back in,
Thanks, dad, I shouted in a spin.
The race was nearly over,
I though I'd win a Rover.
I passed the finish line,
Yes, I shouted, oh, my spine.
Here's the prize, it's a, it's a, it's a baby alien.
Aaaaaaahhhhh my mum screamed.
Never ever am I going back to Space,
As this baby alien is such a disgrace.

Jabbar Shah (10)
William Austin Junior School

ERROR: syntaxerror
OFFENDING COMMAND: 8.2_

STACK:

(5.847 in)
(0 in)
(0 in)
-mark-